Praise for Paula Maust's website,
Expanding the Music Theory Canon

"Congratulations on completing this wonderful project. This is such a significant contribution to the field of music theory."
— Joseph Chi-Sing Siu, University of Maryland Baltimore County

"She's doing what most of us are talking about and not knowing how to do."
— David Forrest, Texas Tech University and President, Texas Society for Music Theory

EXPANDING THE MUSIC THEORY CANON

EXPANDING THE MUSIC THEORY CANON

Inclusive Examples for Analysis from the Common Practice Period

Paula Maust

Clockwise from left to right: Head shots of Amanda Aldridge, Samuel Coleridge-Taylor, Fanny Hensel, José White, Nadia Boulanger, Isabella Colbran, Julie Candeille, and Joseph Bologne. Public domain.

Published by State University of New York Press, Albany

© 2024 State University of New York

All rights reserved

Printed in the United States of America

No part of this book may be used or reproduced in any manner whatsoever without written permission. No part of this book may be stored in a retrieval system or transmitted in any form or by any means including electronic, electrostatic, magnetic tape, mechanical, photocopying, recording, or otherwise without the prior permission in writing of the publisher.

For information, contact State University of New York Press, Albany, NY
www.sunypress.edu

Library of Congress Cataloging-in-Publication Data

Name: Maust, Paula, author.
Title: Expanding the music theory canon : inclusive examples for analysis from the common practice period / Paula Maust.
Description: Albany : State University of New York Press, [2024] | Includes bibliographical references and index.
Identifiers: ISBN 9781438495804 (ebook) | ISBN 9781438495811 (pbk. : alk. paper)
Further information is available at the Library of Congress.

10 9 8 7 6 5 4 3 2 1

To my students, who continuously inspire me to pursue greater knowledge.

CONTENTS

Acknowledgments ix
Editorial Principles xi
Introduction 1
How to Use This Anthology 3

PART I: FUNDAMENTALS

Chapter 1 Major and Minor Scales; Diatonic Modes   11
Chapter 2 Triads and Seventh Chords   19
Chapter 3 Simple Meters   27
Chapter 4 Compound and Asymmetrical Meters   37
Chapter 5 Borrowed Beat Divisions, Polyrhythms, and Hemiolas   45

PART II: EMBELLISHING TONES

Chapter 6   Passing Tones   57
Chapter 7   Neighbor Tones and Incomplete Neighbors   61
Chapter 8   Appoggiaturas and Anticipations   67
Chapter 9   Pedals   71
Chapter 10 Suspensions   77

PART III: HARMONIC PROGRESSIONS

Chapter 11 Cadences   87
Chapter 12 Tonic and Dominant Triads   95
Chapter 13 The Dominant Seventh Chord   101
Chapter 14 The Leading-Tone Triad and Seventh Chord   107
Chapter 15 Predominant Triads and Seventh Chords;
            the Embellishing Subdominant   113

Chapter 16	Second-Inversion Triads	125
Chapter 17	Submediant and Mediant Triads	131
Chapter 18	Secondary Dominants	139
Chapter 19	Augmented Sixth Chords	149
Chapter 20	The Neapolitan	157
Chapter 21	Modal Mixture	161
Chapter 22	Common-Tone Diminished Seventh Chords	171
Chapter 23	Chromatic Mediants	175
Chapter 24	Diatonic and Chromatic Modulation	179
Chapter 25	Sequences	191

PART IV: FORMAL STRUCTURES

Chapter 26	Phrase Structures	205
Chapter 27	Binary Form	213
Chapter 28	Sonata Form	219
Chapter 29	Minuet and Trio	245
Chapter 30	Rondo and Sonata-Rondo Forms	249
Chapter 31	Theme and Variations; Ground Bass	287
Chapter 32	Fugue	299
Chapter 33	Large Ternary Form	303
Composer Biographies		313
Bibliography		337
Index		341

ACKNOWLEDGMENTS

I am profoundly grateful to Jeffrey Martin, a music composition student at the University of Maryland, Baltimore County (UMBC), for his beautiful and detail-oriented work engraving the musical examples in this anthology. I would also like to thank UMBC for awarding me the 2021 Adjunct Faculty Excellence Award, which partially funded those engravings. Generous financial support was also provided by a 2023 Peabody Career Development Grant and a 2023 Subvention Grant from the Society for Music Theory. Additionally, Mark Janello, my friend and colleague at the Peabody Institute of the Johns Hopkins University, offered advice at many points in the process of compiling this anthology.

Much of my research has been made possible by the digitization and free online availability of public domain scores on the International Music Score Library Project (IMSLP). Digitized collections of historical manuscripts at the Bibliothèque nationale de France and the Museo internazionale e biblioteca della musica di Bologna were also tremendously helpful. Paul Allen Sommerfeld and several other music librarians at the Library of Congress processed my numerous requests for obscure scores by late-nineteenth and early-twentieth-century Black American women and assisted with locating several of the images of composers.

I am also grateful to the SUNY Press staff for their commitment and great care in producing this anthology. In particular, I would like to thank my editor, Richard Carlin, for his guidance and belief in the importance of this project.

EDITORIAL PRINCIPLES

The source materials for the musical examples in this anthology include unpublished historical manuscripts, parts, and publications in the public domain. Throughout the anthology, I have corrected any obvious note errors found in the original source materials. I have also unified slurring, articulations, and dynamics, particularly in ensemble works with variances in the original parts. Additionally, I have standardized all beaming to follow current notational conventions. In vocal works, for example, pitches are beamed together by beat, rather than by syllable. Each line of poetry in the vocal works has been capitalized, and slurs have been added to indicate melismas. For consistency and clarity, I have also standardized and modernized accidentals. All figured bass realizations in this anthology are my own; I have added supplemental figured bass symbols as needed for clarity. Any errors in the transcription of these works are my own.

INTRODUCTION

When I taught my first Western classical music theory courses in 2016, I was disheartened by the dearth of musical examples by women and people of color active during the Common Practice Period (c. 1600–1920) in undergraduate textbooks and anthologies.[1] This persistent and widespread omission perpetuates the false historical narratives that either (1) women and people of color were not writing music before the twentieth century or (2) the music they composed is not worthy of serious study. I was determined to begin correcting the narrative in my own courses and started collecting musical examples by historical women and people of color from Western Europe and the Americas. Those examples form the core of this anthology, and since 2016 I have used them at a regional public university with a liberal arts emphasis, a private Research 1 university, and a major conservatory. When we analyze each example in class, I also share a brief biography and image of the composer to further deepen my students' engagement with these historical figures. Broadening the representation of compositional voices is tremendously impactful to many students today, as evidenced by a study I conducted in 2021. The majority of participants aged eighteen to thirty-five indicated that studying Western classical music by a historical composer who shared an underrepresented aspect of their identity was a critical, career-defining moment.[2]

This anthology contains 255 musical examples organized by Western classical music theory topics and specifically curated to be used in Advanced Placement courses, the undergraduate core curriculum, elective courses, and graduate review courses. Most of the sixty-seven composers whose works are featured in this anthology have not previously had their music included in a Western classical music theory textbook or anthology. In particular, I have incorporated a number of examples by women of color

---

1. The term *Common Practice Period* is problematic because it can imply that music from any other time or place is somehow "uncommon." It is not my intention for this anthology to promote such an idea. However, Common Practice Period remains the most well-known term in our field for describing the type of music found in this anthology—specifically music written in the Western classical style from c. 1600 to 1920.

2. Paula Maust, "Racism and Sexism Remain Pervasive in Western Classical Music Instruction," *Journal of the International Alliance for Women in Music* 27 no. 1 (Spring 2021): 21–23. This study was inspired in part by Philip A. Ewell's groundbreaking "Music Theory and the White Racial Frame," *Music Theory Online* 26 no. 2 (September 2020).

and composers from the Americas. I have also purposefully included a significant number of vocal works and pieces from the seventeenth and early eighteenth centuries, since many music theory textbooks predominantly utilize instrumental examples written between c. 1730 and 1900. Finally, the known professional accomplishments of each composer are highlighted in biographies at the end of the anthology, each of which is accompanied by an image of the composer. For composers with no definitive surviving image, I have instead featured the cover page of one of their musical scores. Further musical examples can be found at https://www.expandingthemusictheorycanon.com, an open education resource I launched in January 2021 with users in sixty-nine countries.

A canon is by definition exclusive, and it is certainly not possible to study the music of every historical composer in an undergraduate core curriculum. Expanding the canon to include a more diverse array of voices does not mean that the works of already established canonical composers need to be erased. Rather, we can teach works from the canon alongside works such as the ones in this anthology, thereby giving our students a much more well-rounded and accurate educational experience. The sixty-seven composers in this anthology represent a small subset of the countless women and people of color who were writing Western classical music during the Common Practice Period. Indeed, there is an expansive wealth of music waiting to be uncovered for use in performance as well as scholarly and pedagogical settings. As the field of Western classical music evolves in the twenty-first century, we need audience members, composers, ensemble managers, conductors, scholars, and performers who are able to advocate for a more equitable and expansive discipline. Perhaps this anthology can be a small step in that direction.

HOW TO USE THIS ANTHOLOGY

FOR THE INSTRUCTOR

This anthology contains 255 musical examples that are organized by Western classical music theory topic, and it is specifically designed to be used as a supplement to existing harmony and form textbooks. The examples are drawn from the works of women and/or people of color writing in the Western classical tradition during the Common Practice Period (c. 1600–1920). As such, each example can be used in a wide variety of Advanced Placement, undergraduate, and graduate review music theory curricula. Chapters 1–26 contain excerpts of larger works, while chapters 27–33 contain nineteen complete scores for analysis. The examples in each chapter are arranged to begin with the simplest and proceed to the most complex. Each chapter also includes a set of analysis questions that are specifically designed to walk students through score analysis in a series of graduated steps. These questions are tailored to the level of an analyst studying each concept for the first time. The biographies at the end of the anthology highlight the known professional accomplishments of each composer, thereby inserting these underrepresented figures into the historical narrative of Western classical music's development.

The following tables illustrate which examples from this anthology are best suited to each chapter of seven widely used undergraduate music theory textbooks.

Table H.1. Steven G. Laitz and Michael R. Callahan, *The Complete Musician*, 5th ed. Author provided.

Chapter	Suggested Anthology Examples	Chapter	Suggested Anthology Examples
1A	1.1–6	17	18.1–11
1B	3.1–10; 4.1–9; 5.1–4, 6–7	18	24.1–5
3	2.1–9	19	25.1–12
4	6.1–2; 7.1–2	20	27.1–5; 31.1–3
5	11.1–8; 12.1–3	21	21.1–9; 23.1–4
6	13.1–2	22	24.6–10
7	12.4–8; 14.1–4	23	20.1–5
8	13.3–10; 14.5–8	24	19.1–8
9	11.8; 15.1–11	25	29.1; 33.1
10	6.1, 5–6; 7.3–7; 8.1–4; 9.1–7; 10.1–3, 5–12	26	30.1–4
11	11.12–13; 15.19–20; 16.1–11	27	28.1–3; 30.5
12	15.12–18	28	22.1–5; 24.11–12
13	11.9–11; 17.1–5; 31.2	29	25.13–14
14	17.6–9	30	1.5–6
15	26.1–3, 7	32	4.7–9; 5.5
16	26.4–6, 10–12		

Table H.2. Stefan Kostka, Dorothy Payne, and Byron Almén, *Tonal Harmony*, 8th ed. Author provided.

Chapter	Suggested Anthology Examples	Chapter	Suggested Anthology Examples
1	1.1–4	16	18.1–6
2	3.1–10; 4.1–6; 5.1–4	17	18.7–11; 25.3, 9, 11
3	2.1–9	18	24.1–5
4	12.1–8; 13.1–10; 14.1–8; 15.1–20; 17.1–9	19	24.6–8; 25.2, 4–7, 12
7	12.1–8; 13.1–10; 14.1–4; 15.1–9; 17.1–9; 25.1	20	27.1–5; 28.1–3; 29.1, 30.1–5, 33.1
8	12.4–8; 13.3, 9; 14.1–4; 15.4, 7–9	21	20.1–5; 21.1–9; 24.9–10
9	16.1–11	22	19.1–8
10	11.1–13; 26.1–7, 12	23	24.11–12
12	6.1–6; 7.1–3; 10.1–12	24	22.1–5
13	7.4–7; 8.1–4; 9.1–7	25	23.1–4; 25.13–14
14	13.1–10	26	1.5–6; 4.7–9; 5.5–7
15	14.5–8; 15.12–18; 25.2, 8		

Table H.3. L. Poundie Burstein and Joseph N. Straus, *Concise Introduction to Tonal Harmony*, 2nd ed. Author provided.

Chapter	Suggested Anthology Examples	Chapter	Suggested Anthology Examples
0	3.1–10; 4.1–6; 5.3–4	22	25.1–2, 8, 10
1	1.1–4	23	16.5–11
3	2.1–9	24	11.1–8; 12.5–8; 13.3–10; 14.1–8
6	11.1–8	25	18.1
7	6.1–2, 4–5; 7.1–2; 8.1–4; 10.1–12	26	18.2–11
9	12.1–3	27	24.2–3, 5
10	11.1–3, 5; 13.1–2	28	24.1, 4
11	12.4–8	29	21.1–9
12	13.3, 7, 9	30	20.1–5
13	13.4–6, 8, 10; 14.1–4	31	19.1–7
14	15.1–3, 6–11, 13–14	32	19.8; 22.1–5
15	16.1–4	33	25.3–7, 9, 11–14
16	11.12–13; 15.19–20	34	24.6–12
17	14.5–8	35	26.4–6, 9
18	11.8; 15.4–5, 12, 15–18	36	26.1–3, 7, 10–12
19	11.9–11; 17.1–5	37	27.1–5
20	6.1–6; 7.1–7; 9.1–7; 10.1–12	38	29.1; 30.1–4; 33.1
21	17.6–9	39	28.1–3; 30.5

Table H.4. Edward Aldwell, Carl Schachter, and Allen Cadwallader, *Harmony & Voice Leading*, 5th ed. Author provided.

Unit	Suggested Anthology Examples	Unit	Suggested Anthology Examples
1	1.1–6; 6.2; 7.1–2	20	16.1–11
3	3.1–10; 4.1–9; 5.6–7; 6.1, 4–5; 8.1–4; 10.1–6	21	6.1–6; 7.1–7; 8.1–2
4	2.1–9	22	8.3–4; 9.1–7; 10.1–12
7	11.1–7; 12.1–3; 13.1–2	23	14.4–8
8	12.4–8; 14.1–3	24	21.1–9
9	13.3–10	25	15.17–18; 25.2, 8
10	15.1–3, 5–11	26	18.1–11; 25.3, 9, 11
11	11.1, 3; 16.1–4	27	24.1–5; 25.4–7, 12
12	11.8; 15.4; 17.1–3, 5	29	20.1–5
13	15.12–18	30	19.1–8
14	11.9–13; 15.19–20; 17.4	31	22.1–5
15	18.1; 24.2–3	32	25.11, 13–14
16	17.6–9; 24.1; 27.1, 5	33	24.6–12; 25.13–14
18	25.1, 10, 12		

Table H.5. Jane Piper Clendinning and Elizabeth West Marvin, *The Musician's Guide to Theory and Analysis*, 4th ed. Author provided.

Chapter	Suggested Anthology Examples	Chapter	Suggested Anthology Examples
2	3.1–10; 5.7	18	26.1–7, 10–12
3	1.1–2, 5	19	18.1, 8
4	4.1–6; 5.1–6	20	18.2–7, 9–11
5	1.3–4, 6	21	25.1, 3, 8–11
7	2.1–3	22	24.1–8
8	2.4–9	23	27.1–5; 29.1
10	6.1, 3, 5; 7.1–2; 10.3, 6, 10–11	24	32.1
11	6.1–6; 7.1–3; 10.1–6	25	31.1–3
12	11.1–8; 12.1–8	26	21.1–9; 23.1–4
13	13.1–10; 15.1–18	27	19.1–8; 20.1–5
14	15.19–20; 16.1–11; 17.1–5	28	22.1–5; 24.9–12; 25.2, 4–7, 12–14
15	11.9–13; 17.6–9; 25.1	30	28.1–3
16	6.1–6; 7.1–7; 8.1–4; 9.1–7; 10.1–12	31	30.1–5; 33.1
17	14.1–8	35	4.7–9

Table H.6. Miguel A. Roig-Francolí, *Harmony in Context*, 3rd ed. Author provided.

Chapter	Suggested Anthology Examples	Chapter	Suggested Anthology Examples
B	3.1–10; 4.1–9; 5.1–7	15	14.5–8; 15.12–18
C	1.1–6	16	25.1–2, 8, 10
D	2.1–9	17	18.1, 3
E	11.1–8	18	18.2, 4–6; 25.3, 9, 11
2	11.1–8; 12.1–3	19	18.7–11
3	11.12–13; 15.1–3, 19–20	20	24.1–5; 25.2, 4, 5–7, 12; 26.3
4	12.4–8; 15.4	21	27.1–5; 29.1; 31.1–3; 33.1
5	15.5–11	22	32.1
6	6.1–6; 7.1–7; 8.1–4; 9.1–7; 10.1–12	23	21.1–9
7	16.1–11	24	20.1–5
8	13.1–10	25	19.1–8
9	14.1–4	26	24.9–12
10	11.1–13	27	22.1–5; 23.1–4; 24.6–8
11	26.1–7, 10–12	28	28.1–3; 30.1–4
14	17.1–9	29	25.13–14

Table H.7. Bruce Benward and Marilyn Saker, *Music in Theory and Practice*, 10th ed. Author provided.

Chapter	Suggested Anthology Examples	Chapter	Suggested Anthology Examples
1	3.1–10; 4.1–9; 5.1–7	16	27.1–5
2	1.1–6	17	27.3–5; 29.1; 33.1
4	2.1–9	18	3.10; 10.3–4, 6–7, 9–11
5	6.1–6; 7.1–7; 8.1–4; 9.1–7; 10.1–12; 11.1–13	20	32.1
6	26.1–3, 7, 12	21	21.1–9
9	12.1–8; 14.1–4; 15.1–11; 16.1–11; 17.1–5	22	20.1–5
10	14.1–4; 16.1–4; 17.1–9; 25.1	23	19.1–8
11	13.1–10	24	31.1–3
12	14.5–8	25	28.1–3
13	15.12–18	26	30.1–5
14	18.1–11	29	23.1–4; 24.6–8
15	24.1–12; 26.3	30	21.1–9; 22.1–5; 24.6–12

FOR THE STUDENT

Analyzing musical scores is a practice you will continue to refine throughout your musical education and beyond. Score analysis can be as simple as identifying pitches and meters or as complex as discussing the nuances of harmonic progressions, melodic embellishments, harmonic rhythm, text setting, phrase structure, texture, timbre, and the form of entire pieces. Close study of a musical score can help you hone your musical interpretations, inspire your original compositions, and/or provide insight into your perspective as a listener or scholar. The pieces in this anthology demonstrate the richness of contributors to Western classical music's development during the Common Practice Period (c. 1600–1920). Since many of the sixty-seven composers introduced in this anthology are not well-known, I encourage you to read the composer biographies at the end of the book in order to more deeply engage with the music's historical context.

PART I
FUNDAMENTALS

1

Major and Minor Scales; Diatonic Modes

This chapter presents major, minor, and chromatic scales and several diatonic modes. Examples 1.1–1.5 contain major, minor, and chromatic scales, and example 1.6 includes multiple types of scales and diatonic modes.

ANALYSIS QUESTIONS

1. What scale(s) and/or diatonic mode(s) occurs in each example?
2. What is the pattern of half and whole steps in each scale or diatonic mode?
3. What is the tonic or starting pitch for each scale or diatonic mode?
4. How is the ascending melodic minor scale different from the descending melodic minor scale?
5. Are any accidentals used to create each scale or diatonic mode?
6. In example 1.6, identify any scalar pitch collections that cannot be defined as a diatonic mode or a major, minor, or chromatic scale.
    a. What is the pattern of half and whole steps in each scalar pitch collection?

b. What scales and/or diatonic modes are most similar to each scalar pitch collection?

c. Divide each scalar collection into two tetrachords and compare them to the tetrachords found in the diatonic modes and the major, minor, and chromatic scales. Which two scales and/or diatonic modes may have been combined to create each scalar pitch collection?

Major and Minor Scales; Diatonic Modes 13

1.1. Je l'ai reçu

Hortense de Beauharnais (1783-1837)

1.2. Deux élégies, Op. 18: Partie I

Teresa Carreño (1853-1917)

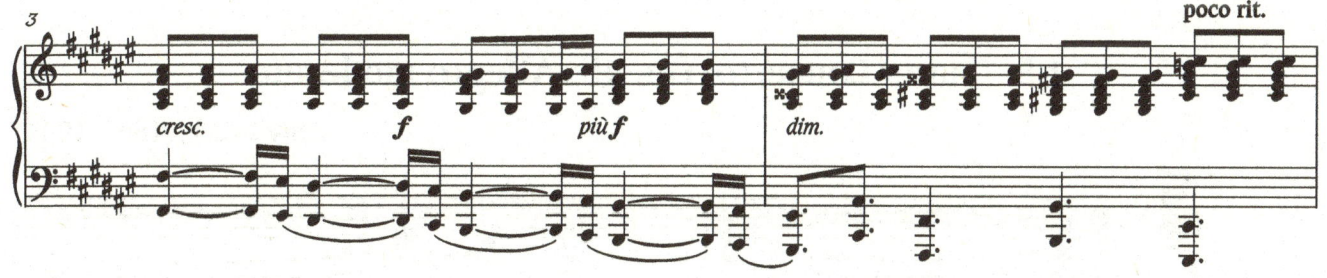

1.3. Lesson No. 1: Minuetto

Elizabeth Turner (1700-1756)

1.4. L'orage

Hortense de Beauharnais (1783-1837)

1.5. Piano Concerto, Op. 45: Allegro moderato

Amy Beach (1867-1944)

Major and Minor Scales; Diatonic Modes   15

1.6. Étude No. 2, Op. 42

Louise Farrenc (1804-1875)

2

Triads and Seventh Chords

This chapter presents the qualities and inversions of triads and seventh chords in straightforward examples with either a block chord accompaniment or arpeggiated chords in the lowest voice. Examples 2.1–2.3 are composed exclusively of triads, and example 2.5 contains only seventh chords. All other examples in the chapter include both triads and seventh chords.

ANALYSIS QUESTIONS

1. What is the root of each chord?

2. What qualities of thirds are used to create each chord?

3. What is the quality of the interval between the root and the fifth of each chord?

4. What is the quality of the interval between the root and the seventh of each seventh chord?

5. What is the quality of each chord?

6. What is the inversion of each chord?

7. Is each chord presented as a block chord or a melodic arpeggiation?

8. Identify any embellishing tones. How do you know these pitches are not part of the chord?

9. What are the musical clues that help you to identify when a new chord has begun?

10. What is the harmonic rhythm for each example?

2.1. Hochzeits-Marsch, Op. 42

Josephine Lang (1815-1880)

2.2. Air italien, Op. 170

Cécile Chaminade (1857-1944)

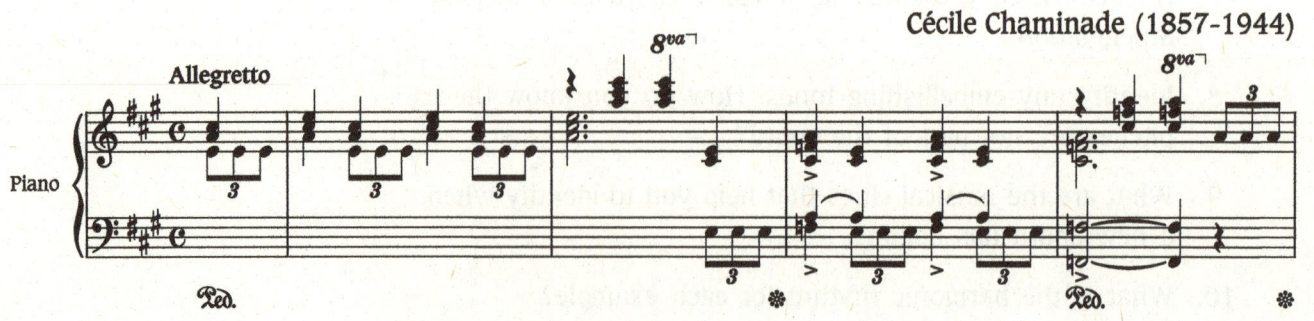

2.3. L'attente

Hortense de Beauharnais (1783-1837)

2.4. Les caractères de l'Amour: Prologue, Air pour les genies

Mademoiselle Duval (1718-after 1775)

2.5. Sometimes I feel like a Motherless Child

Harry Thacker Burleigh (1866-1949)

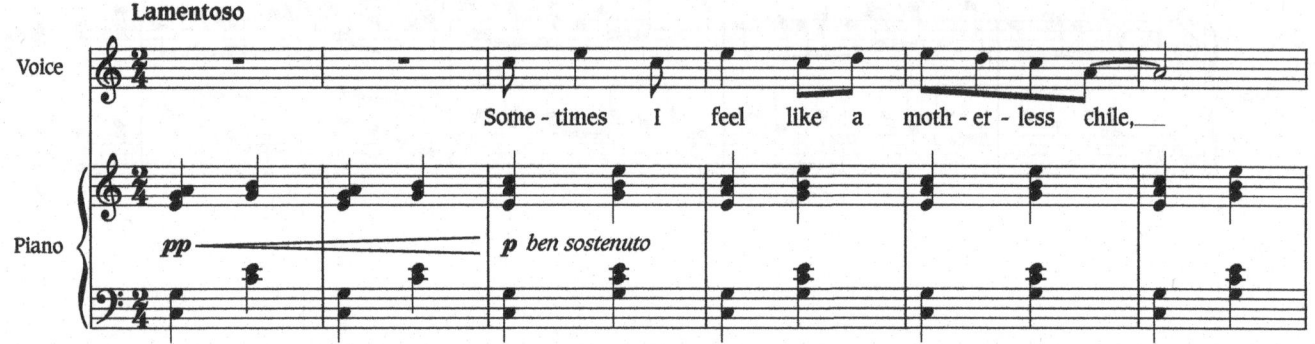

2.6. Unruhiger Schlaf

Louise Reichardt (1779-1826)

2.7. Four Characteristic Waltzes, Op. 22: Valse de la Reine

Samuel Coleridge-Taylor (1875-1912)

2.8. Frühzeitiger Frühling, Op. 6

Josephine Lang (1815-1880)

1. Ta - ge der Won - ne, Kommt ihr so bald?

Triads and Seventh Chords

2.9. Piano Trio, Op. 17: Scherzo

Clara Schumann (1819-1896)

3

Simple Meters

This chapter presents duple, triple, and quadruple simple meters. All examples contain the rhythmic durations of both the beat and the beat division, except example 3.8, which is primarily composed of beat subdivisions. Smaller units of subdivision are illustrated most prominently in examples 3.2 and 3.9, and irregular beat divisions occur in example 3.7.

ANALYSIS QUESTIONS

1. How many beats are in each measure?
2. What is the rhythmic duration of the beat?
3. What is the rhythmic duration of the beat division?
4. What is the rhythmic duration of the beat subdivision?
5. Identify any rhythmic durations that are smaller than the beat subdivision. How do these rhythmic durations relate to the beat?
6. What is the rhythmic function of the eighth note in each meter in example 3.1?
7. Does the beaming in each example clearly reflect the meter? Why, or why not?
8. Identify all dotted rhythms. How does a dot change the duration of a note in simple meters?
9. Identify all ties. What does a tie do to the duration of the notes it connects?

10. Why are both ties and dotted notes needed to clearly depict the meter in example 3.10?

11. Which examples in this chapter contain syncopation? How is the syncopation created?

3.1. Danse des lutins

Henriette Renié (1875-1956)

3.2. Etude No. 1, Op. 33

José White (1836-1918)

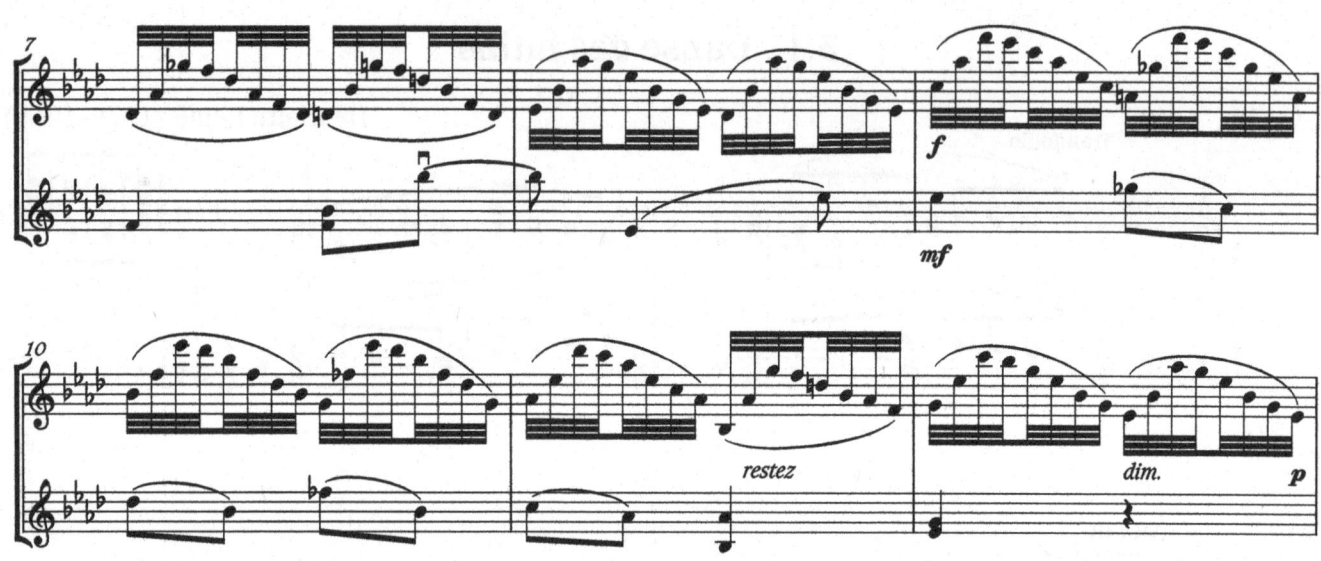

3.3. String Quartet No. 4, Op. 1: Allegro moderato

Joseph Bologne (1745-1799)

3.4. Sonata No. 2, Op. 1: Allegro

Anna Bon (c.1738-after 1769)

3.5. Carlos Gomes

Allegro vivace

Chiquinha Gonzaga (1847-1935)

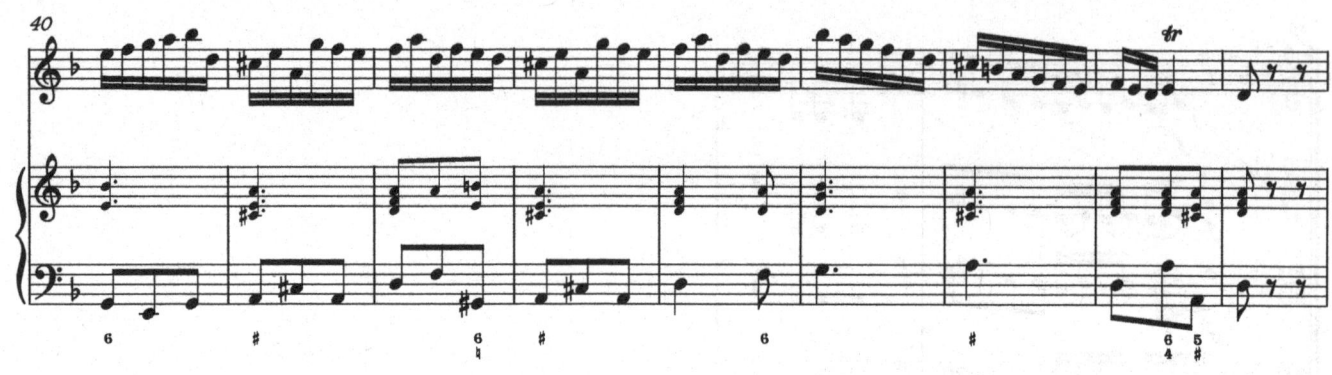

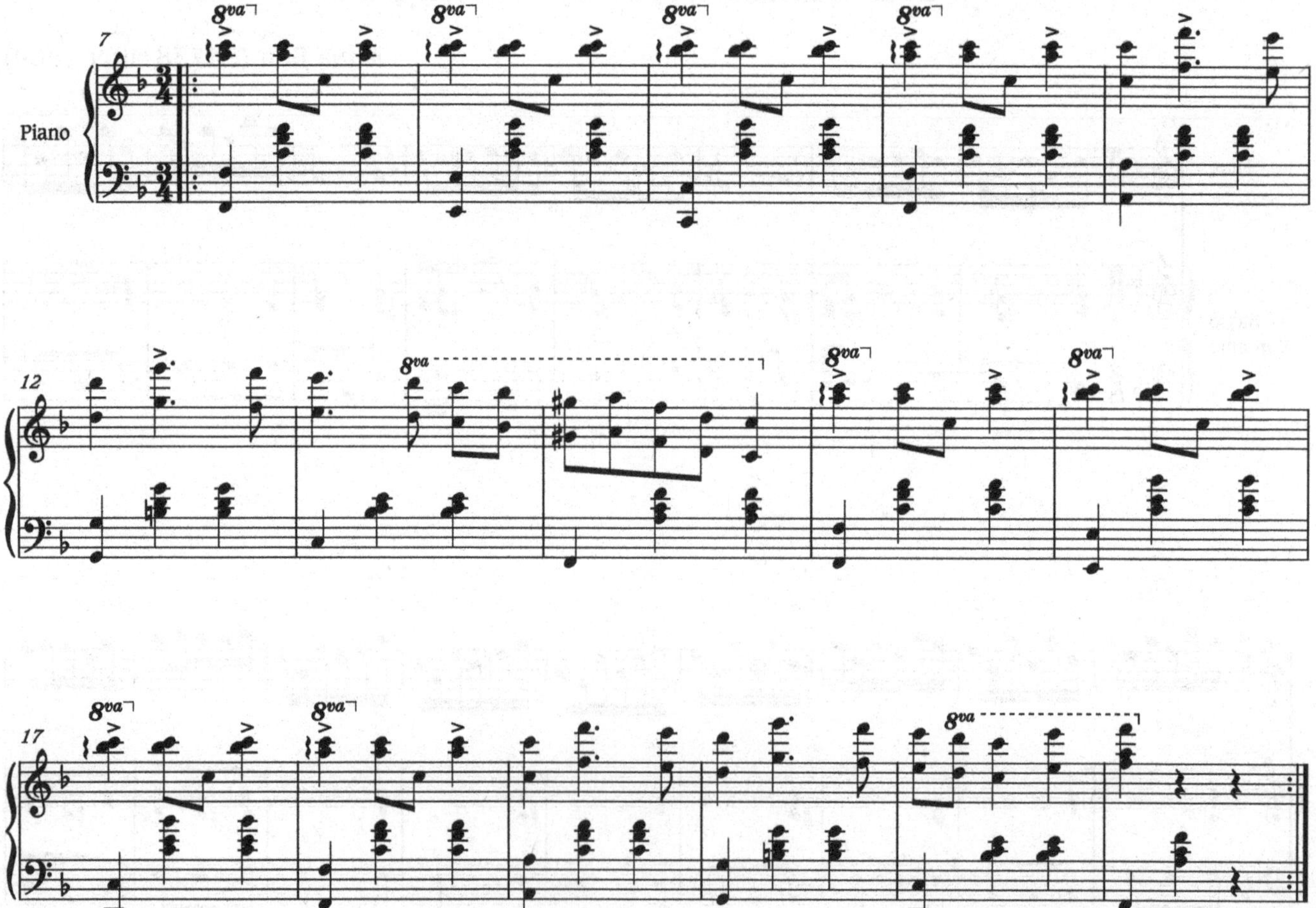

3.6. Arie: All' mein Leben bist du

Josephine Lang (1815-1880)

3.7. Carnival: Pierrette

Amanda Aldridge (1866-1956)

3.8. In the Bottoms: Prelude: Night

Robert Nathaniel Dett (1882-1943)

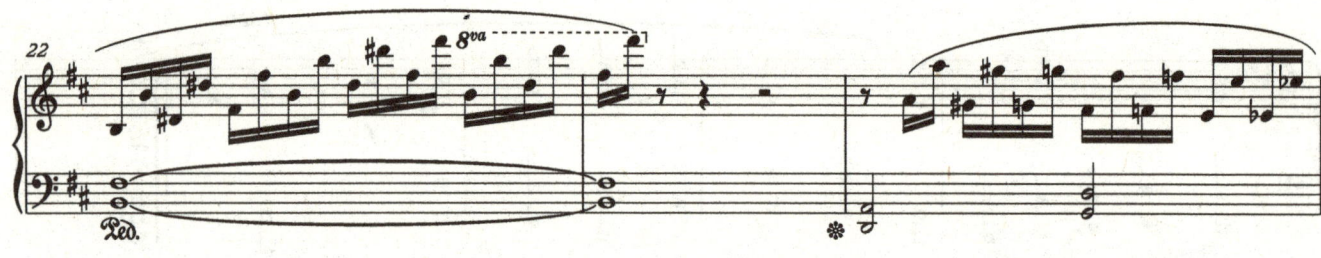

3.9. Six morceaux de salon, Op. 26: Un bal en rêve

Teresa Carreño (1853-1917)

3.10. Cinta di fior un giorno

Maddalena Casulana (c.1544-c.1590)

4

Compound and Asymmetrical Meters

This chapter presents duple, triple, and quadruple compound meters and asymmetrical meters. Examples 4.2–4.6, 4.8, and 4.9 are composed primarily of beat divisions; beat subdivisions occur in examples 4.4, 4.5, and 4.8. Examples 4.3 and 4.8 also include borrowed divisions, and example 4.3 contains a polyrhythm. For additional examples of polyrhythms and borrowed divisions, see chapter 5.

ANALYSIS QUESTIONS

1. How many beats are in each measure?

2. What is the rhythmic duration of the beat?

3. What is the rhythmic duration of the beat division?

4. What is the rhythmic duration of the beat subdivision?

5. Does the beaming in each example clearly reflect the meter? Why, or why not?

6. Identify all ties. What does a tie do to the duration of the notes it connects?

7. Which examples in this chapter contain syncopation? How is the syncopation created?

4.1. String Quartet: Final

Germaine Tailleferre (1892-1983)

4.2. Vaters Klage

Louise Reichardt (1779-1826)

1. Es ste - hen drei Stern' am Him - mel, Die blick - en trau - rig her - ab; Zu Ber - koch an der

4.3. Violin Sonata, Op. 25: Più lento molto sostenuto

Clara Kathleen Rogers (1844-1931)

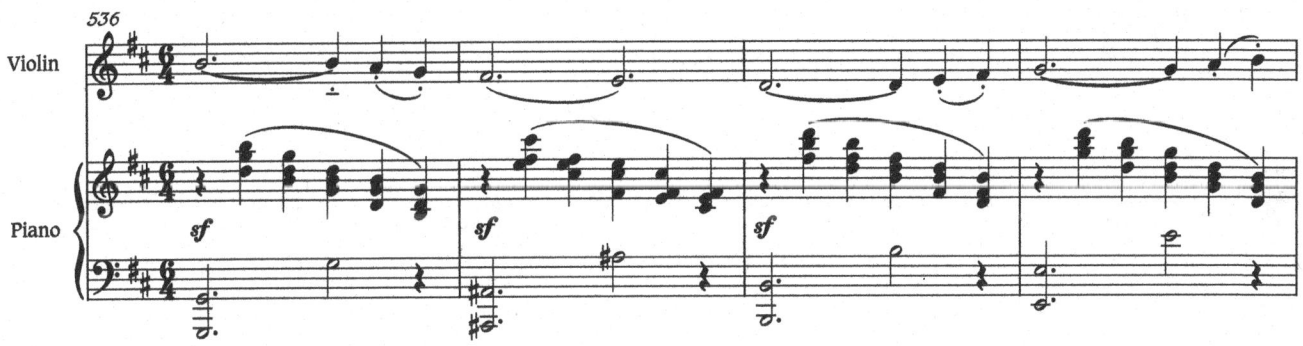

4.4. Che si può fare

Barbara Strozzi (1619-1677)

4.5. Trio for Harp, Violin, and Cello: Andante

Henriette Renié (1875-1956)

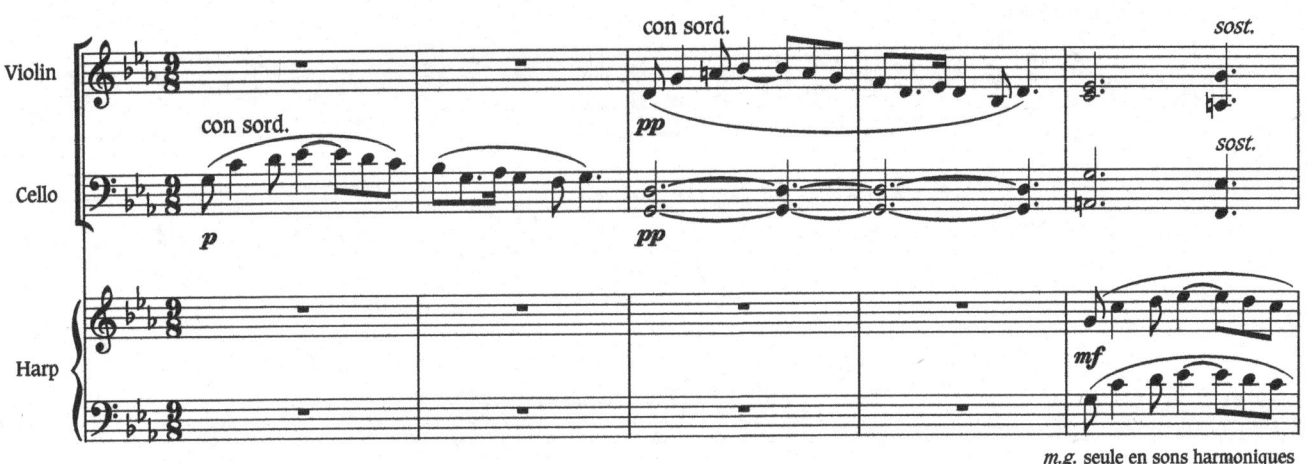

4.6. Trois morceaux de salon, Op. 28: Un rêve en mer

Teresa Carreño (1853–1917)

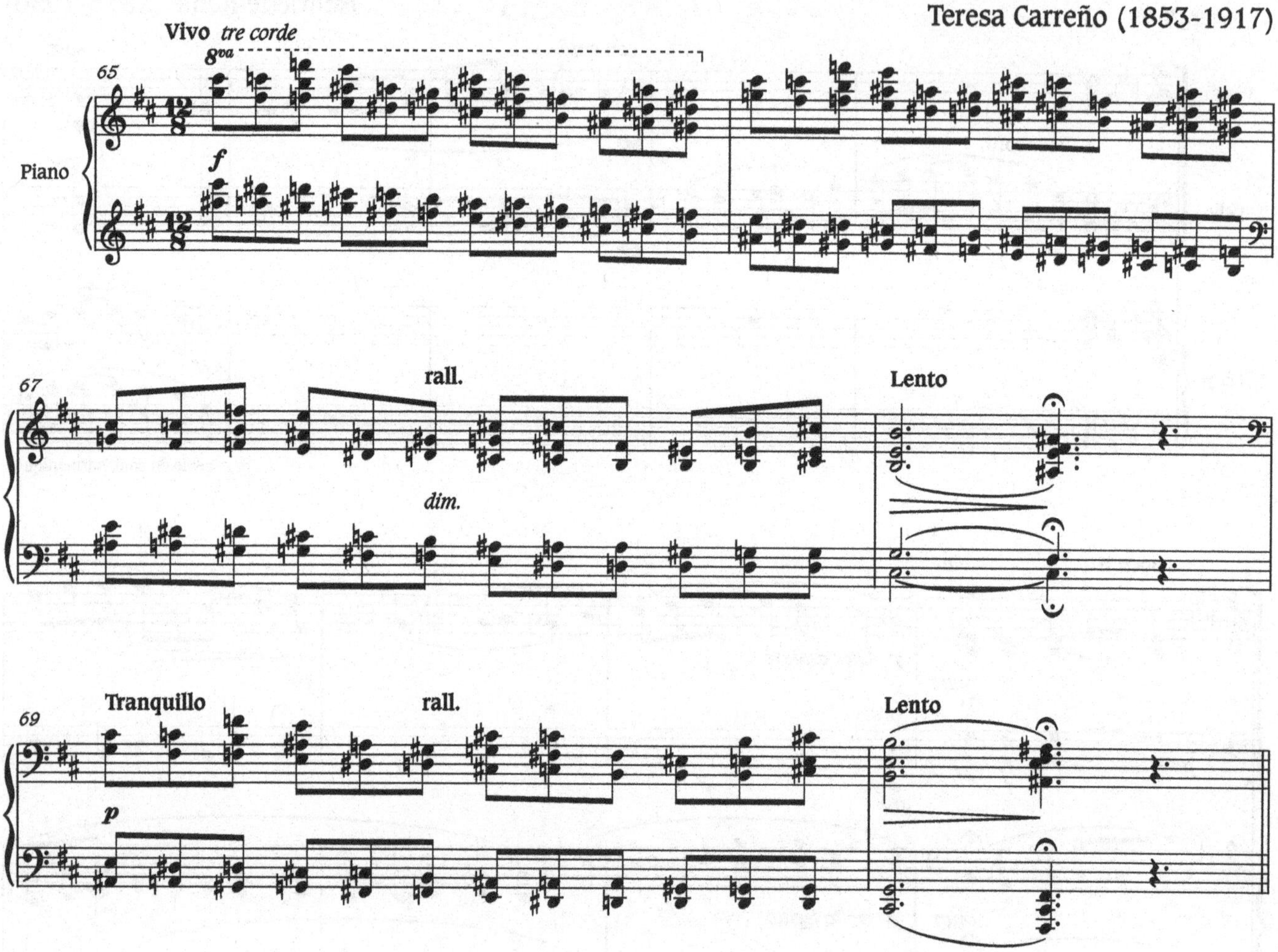

4.7. Three Pieces for Cello and Piano: No. 3

Nadia Boulanger (1887–1979)

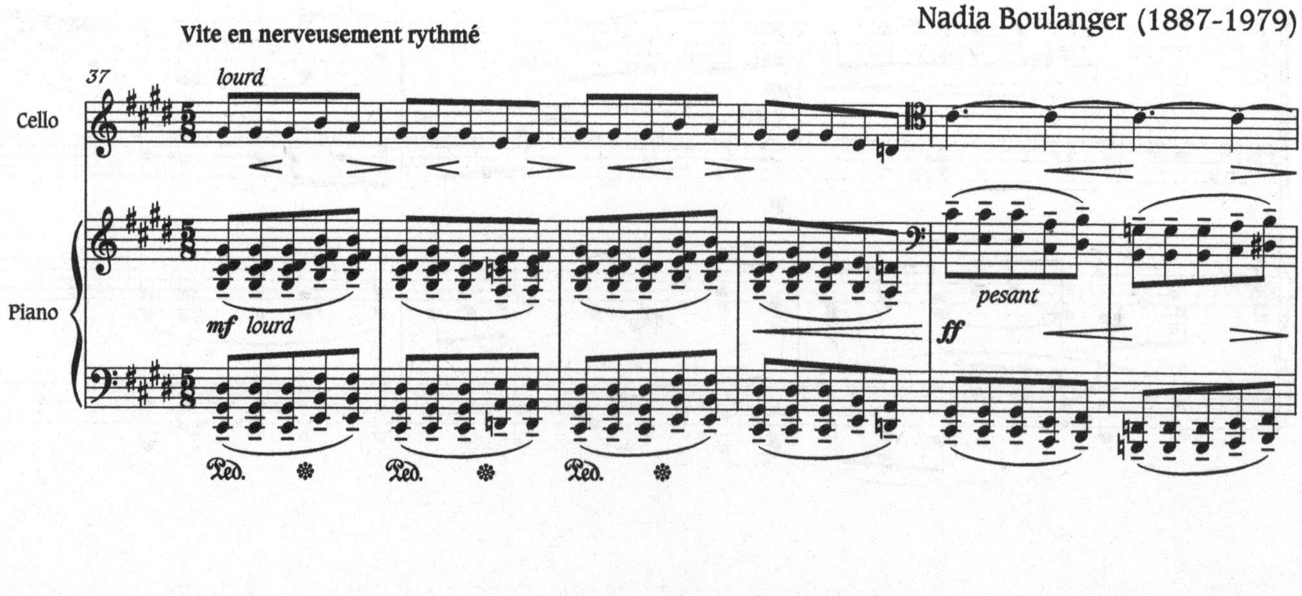

4.8. Fantasiestücke, Op. 5: Serenade

Samuel Coleridge-Taylor (1875-1912)

4.9. Prelude No. 4, Op. 15

Marion Bauer (1882-1955)

5

Borrowed Beat Divisions, Polyrhythms, and Hemiolas

This chapter presents borrowed beat divisions, polyrhythms, and hemiolas in simple and compound meters. Examples 5.1–5.5 contain borrowed beat divisions and polyrhythms, and hemiolas occur in examples 5.6 and 5.7.

ANALYSIS QUESTIONS

1. What are the rhythmic durations of the beat and the beat division?

2. Where do borrowed beat divisions occur?

3. How do the borrowed beat divisions work in each meter?

4. Which meters are the borrowed beat divisions from?

5. Could examples 5.3 and 5.5 be rewritten in a compound meter? If so, which compound meter would you choose, and why?

6. If you rewrite examples 5.3 and 5.5 in a compound meter, which rhythmic durations would become the borrowed beat divisions? What borrowed beat divisions would they become?

7. Where do polyrhythms occur?

8. What two meters are being juxtaposed when the polyrhythms occur?

9. Where do hemiolas occur?

10. How do the hemiolas disrupt the meter?

Borrowed Beat Divisions, Polyrhythms, and Hemiolas

5.1. The Clover Blossoms, Op. 10

Clara Kathleen Rogers (1844-1931)

5.2. Deux élégies, Op. 18: Partie!

Teresa Carreño (1853-1917)

5.3. Blick' nach oben

Josephine Lang (1815-1880)

Borrowed Beat Divisions, Polyrhythms, and Hemiolas   49

5.4. Ballade, Op. 4

Samuel Coleridge-Taylor (1875-1912)

50 Expanding the Music Theory Canon

5.5. Erinnerung ans Schicksal

Maria Theresia von Paradis (1759-1824)

5.6. Violin Sonata No. 2: Presto

Élisabeth Jacquet de la Guerre (1665–1729)

5.7. O sylvæ, ò montes, ò garruli fontes, Op. 11

Isabella Leonarda (1620-1704)

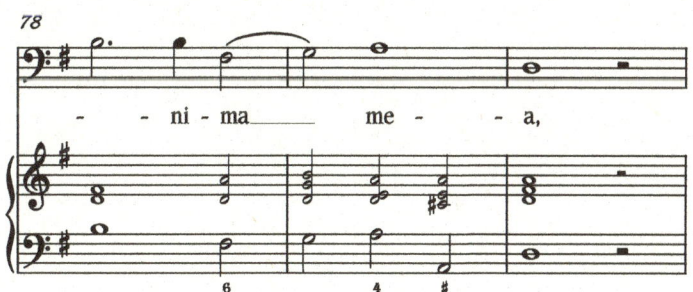

PART II
EMBELLISHING TONES

6

Passing Tones

This chapter presents unaccented, accented, diatonic, and chromatic passing tones in straightforward examples with either a block chord accompaniment or arpeggiated chords in the lowest voice.

ANALYSIS QUESTIONS

1. Identify each harmony or chord. What musical clues help you to determine which pitches are chord tones and which pitches are embellishing tones?

2. What is the harmonic rhythm for each example?

3. Is each passing tone accented or unaccented?

4. Is each passing tone diatonic or chromatic?

5. What other embellishing tones can you identify in this chapter?

6. Are these other embellishing tones accented or unaccented?

7. Are these other embellishing tones diatonic or chromatic?

6.1. Le prisonnier

Hortense de Beauharnais (1783-1837)

6.2. A Collection of New Cotillions: Ford

Francis Johnson (1792-1844)

6.3. Sonata No. 2: Aria con variatione

Joseph Bologne (1745-1799)

6.4. Sonata No. 3: [Allegro]

Joseph Bologne (1745-1799)

6.5. Cinq pièces pour piano: Gai printemps

Mélanie Bonis (1858-1937)

6.6. Ich wollt' ein Sträuslein binden

Louise Reichardt (1779-1826)

7

Neighbor Tones and Incomplete Neighbors

This chapter presents unaccented, accented, diatonic, and chromatic neighbor tones and incomplete neighbors in straightforward examples with either a block chord accompaniment or arpeggiated chords in the lowest voice. For specific examples of appoggiaturas, which are sometimes taught as incomplete neighbors, see chapter 8.

ANALYSIS QUESTIONS

1. Identify each harmony or chord. What musical clues help you to determine which pitches are chord tones and which pitches are embellishing tones?

2. What is the harmonic rhythm for each example?

3. Is each neighbor tone and incomplete neighbor accented or unaccented?

4. Is each neighbor tone and incomplete neighbor diatonic or chromatic?

5. What is the difference between a neighbor tone and an incomplete neighbor?

6. What other embellishing tones can you identify in this chapter?

7. Are these other embellishing tones accented or unaccented?

8. Are these other embellishing tones diatonic or chromatic?

7.1. Carnival: Frolic

Amanda Aldridge (1866-1956)

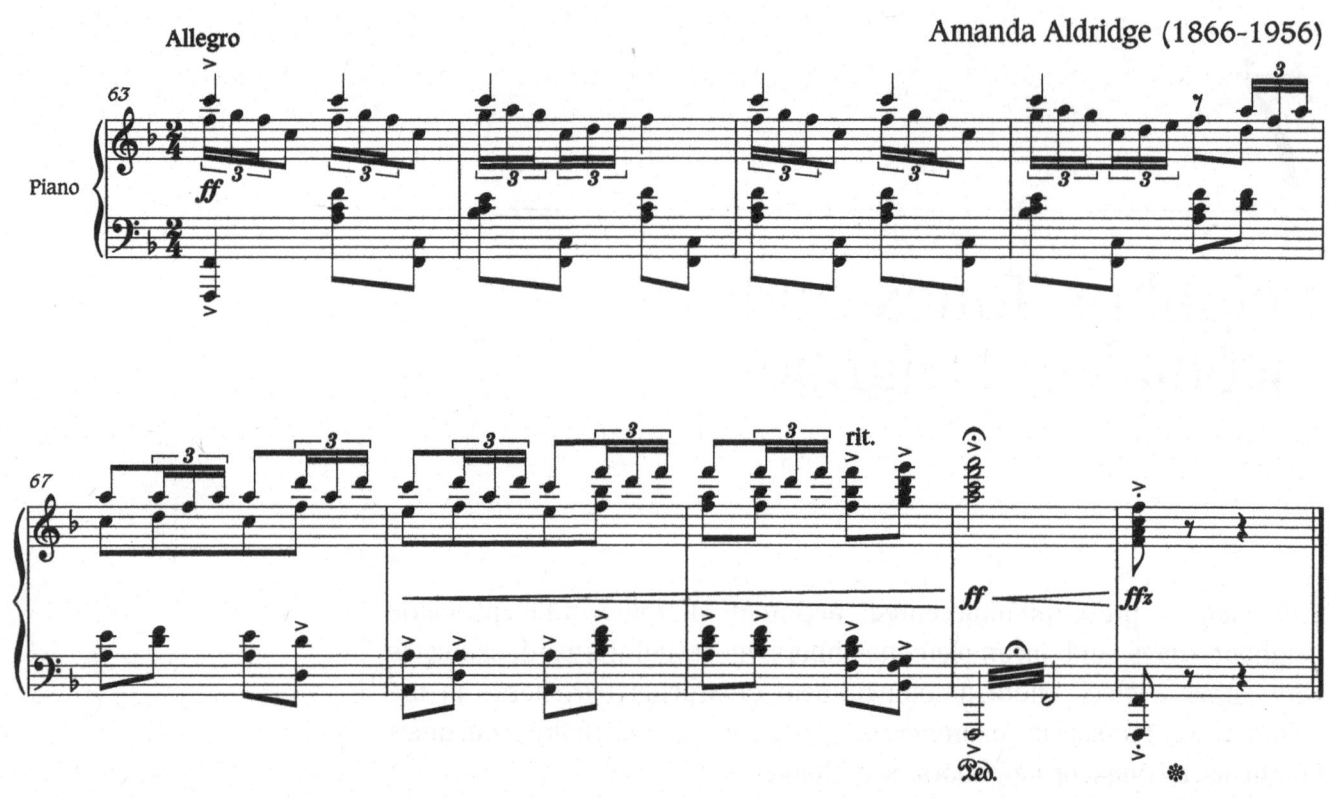

7.2. Sonata No. 6, Op. 16

Isabella Leonarda (1620-1704)

Neighbor Tones and Incomplete Neighbors 63

7.3. Le batelier

Maria Malibrán (1808-1836)

7.4. Douleur et gaîté

Eugène Dédé (1867-1919)

7.5. Più bella Aurora

Isabella Colbran (1785-1845)

7.6. Transports joyeux, Op. 116

Sydney Lambert (1838-1905)

7.7. Sonata No. 2, Op. 1: Largo

Anna Bon (c.1738-after 1769)

8

Appoggiaturas and Anticipations

This chapter presents appoggiaturas and anticipations in straightforward examples with either a block chord accompaniment or arpeggiated chords in the lowest voice. For examples of other types of incomplete neighbors, see chapter 7.

ANALYSIS QUESTIONS

1. Identify each harmony or chord. What musical clues help you to determine which pitches are chord tones and which pitches are embellishing tones?

2. What is the harmonic rhythm of each example?

3. Is each appoggiatura and anticipation accented or unaccented?

4. Is each appoggiatura and anticipation diatonic or chromatic?

5. What other embellishing tones can you identify in this chapter?

6. Are these other embellishing tones accented or unaccented?

7. Are these other embellishing tones diatonic or chromatic?

8.1. Fado das Tricanas de Coimbra

Chiquinha Gonzaga (1847-1935)

8.2. Cuba Libre

Anna Gardner Goodwin (1874-1959)

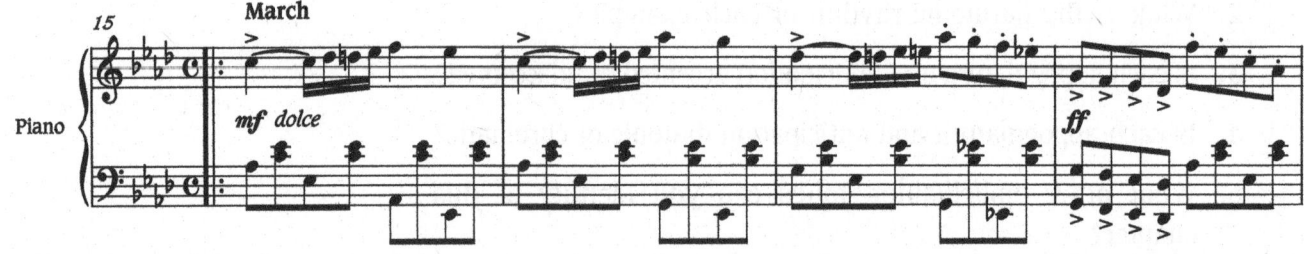

8.3. In April When Prim Roses

Sophia Dussek (b.1775)

8.4. Ubi es ò Domine, Op. 11

Isabella Leonarda (1620-1704)

9

Pedals

This chapter presents examples of tonic and dominant pedals. Examples 9.1 and 9.4 also demonstrate second-inversion pedal triads and can be used as a supplement to examples 16.6–16.9.

ANALYSIS QUESTIONS

1. How do pedals differ from other embellishing tones?
2. Is each pedal a tonic pedal or a dominant pedal?
3. What are the implied harmonies that occur above each pedal?
4. What makes the pedal in example 9.7 different from the other pedals in this chapter?
5. What other embellishing tones can you identify in this chapter?
6. Are these other embellishing tones accented or unaccented?
7. Are these other embellishing tones diatonic or chromatic?

9.1. Hier liegt ein Spielmann begraben

Louise Reichardt (1779-1826)

9.2. Quand mo-té jeune

Maud Cuney Hare (1874-1936)

9.3. Tropical Dance No. 2

Justin Elie (1883-1931)

9.4. Symphony No. 1, Op. 11: Allegro

Joseph Bologne (1745-1799)

9.5. Bijou

Chiquinha Gonzaga (1847-1935)

9.6. Violin Sonata, Op. 25: Allegro

Clara Kathleen Rogers (1844-1931)

9.7. Carillon mystique, Op. 31

Mélanie Bonis (1858-1937)

10

Suspensions

This chapter presents 9-8, 7-6, and 4-3 suspensions; change of bass suspensions; double suspensions; chains of suspensions; and an upward resolving suspension. All examples are composed primarily of diatonic harmonies, although examples 10.4 and 10.10 contain some secondary function.

ANALYSIS QUESTIONS

1. What suspension(s) occurs in each example?

2. Does each suspension have a preparation and a resolution?

3. What is the duration of the resolution?

4. Does each suspension occur in a metrically accented or unaccented position?

5. How is a suspension different from each of the following embellishing tones:

   a. appoggiatura

   b. accented incomplete neighbor

   c. accented passing tone

   d. accented neighbor tone

6. How does a double suspension differ from the cadential 6/4 chord's motion to the dominant?

7. How is a 4-3 suspension related to the cadential 6/4 chord's motion to the dominant?

8. Explain the dual functions of the preparation and resolution notes in a chain of suspensions.

9. What is the difference between a suspension and a retardation?

10.1. Giusto Amor

Louise Reichardt (1779-1826)

10.2. Violin Sonata, Op. 17: Adagio non troppo

Emilie Mayer (1812-1883)

10.3. Ah! Si vous sçaviez mes compagnes

Françoise-Charlotte de Senneterre Ménétou (1679-1745)

10.4. Violin Sonata No. 1: Aria

Élisabeth Jacquet de la Guerre (1665-1729)

10.5. Dort hoch auf jenem Berge

Josephine Lang (1815-1880)

10.6. Chi é costei

Francesca Caccini (1587-after 1641)

10.7. Violin Sonata No. 6: Presto

Élisabeth Jacquet de la Guerre (1665-1729)

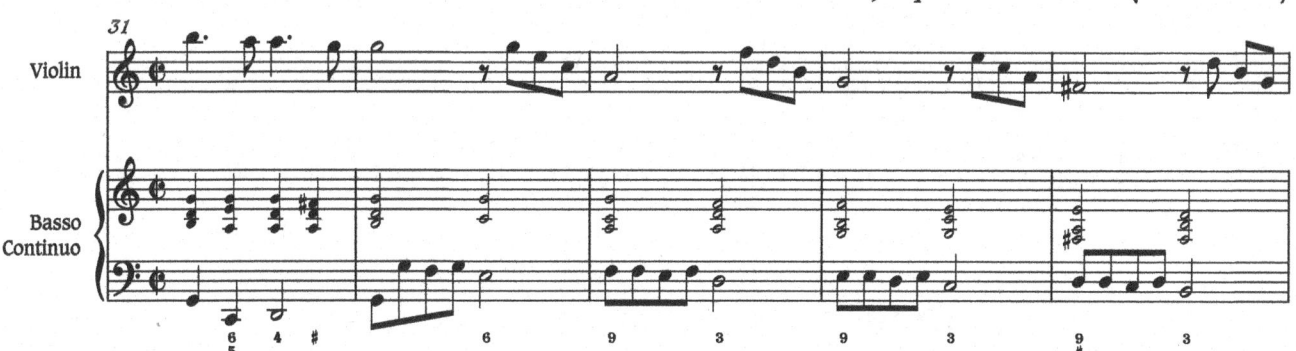

10.8. Sonata No. 4, Op. 2: Rondo allegro assai

Franziska Lebrun (1756-1791)

10.9. Les caractères de l'Amour: Act 1, Scene 1, Air Leandre

Mademoiselle Duval (1718-after 1775)

10.10. Violin Sonata No. 5: Courante

Élisabeth Jacquet de la Guerre (1665-1729)

10.11. Sonata No. 3, Op. 16: Adagio-Presto

Isabella Leonarda (1620-1704)

10.12. Humoreske No. 3, Op. 41

Emilie Mayer (1812-1883)

PART III
HARMONIC PROGRESSIONS

11

Cadences

This chapter presents perfect authentic, imperfect authentic, half, Phrygian half, deceptive, and plagal cadences.

ANALYSIS QUESTIONS

1. What is the key of each example?
2. What type of cadence(s) occurs in each example?
3. What are the differences between a perfect authentic cadence and an imperfect authentic cadence?
4. What is the difference between an authentic cadence and a half cadence?
5. What is a Phrygian half cadence?
6. What chord occurs immediately before each perfect authentic, imperfect authentic, and half cadence?
7. What is the difference between a deceptive cadence and an authentic cadence?
8. What is the difference between a plagal cadence and an authentic cadence?
9. What type of cadence occurs immediately before each plagal cadence?
10. Does each phrase follow the tonal phrase model of tonic–predominant–dominant–tonic?

11.1. Variations on "In my cottage in a wood"

Sophia Dussek (b.1775)

11.2. Schifferlied

Louise Reichardt (1779-1826)

11.3. Sonata in A Major: Tempo di minuetto

Marianna Martines (1744-1812)

11.4. The Three Sighs: Sorrow, Hope, & Bliss

Harriett Abrams (c.1758-1821)

11.5. Sonata in E Major: Allegro

Marianna Martines (1744-1812)

11.6. Der Brautschmuck

Corona Schröter (1751-1802)

11.7. Sonata in G Major: Allegro assai

Marianna Martines (1744-1812)

11.8. Ruisseaux suspendez vôtre cours

Julie Pinel (fl.1710-1737)

11.9. A Smile and a Tear

Harriett Abrams (c.1758-1821)

11.10. So che un sogno è la speranza

Isabella Colbran (1785-1845)

11.11. Sonata No. 5, Op. 1: Rondeau

Franziska Lebrun (1756-1791)

11.12. Variations on "Lewie Gordon"

Sophia Dussek (b.1775)

11.13. Trois morceaux de salon, Op. 25: Le Printemps

Teresa Carreño (1853-1917)

12

Tonic and Dominant Triads

This chapter presents root position and first-inversion tonic and dominant triads in major and minor keys in straightforward examples with either a block chord accompaniment or arpeggiated chords in the lowest voice. All examples are composed entirely of diatonic tonic and dominant triads, with the exception of example 12.7, which also contains a predominant harmony.

ANALYSIS QUESTIONS

1. What is the key of each example?
2. What is the root of each tonic and dominant triad?
3. What is the quality of each tonic and dominant triad?
4. What is the inversion of each tonic and dominant triad?
5. What is the function of each first-inversion tonic and dominant triad?
6. How does the leading tone in each dominant triad resolve?
7. What embellishing tones occur in each example?

12.1. Ne m'oubliez pas!

Hortense de Beauharnais (1783-1837)

1. Vous me quit-tez pour cou-rir à la gloi-re, Mon tris-te coeur sui-vra par-tout vos pas, Al-lez vo-ler au tem-ple de mé-moi-re,

12.2. Hochzeits-Marsch, Op. 42

Josephine Lang (1815-1880)

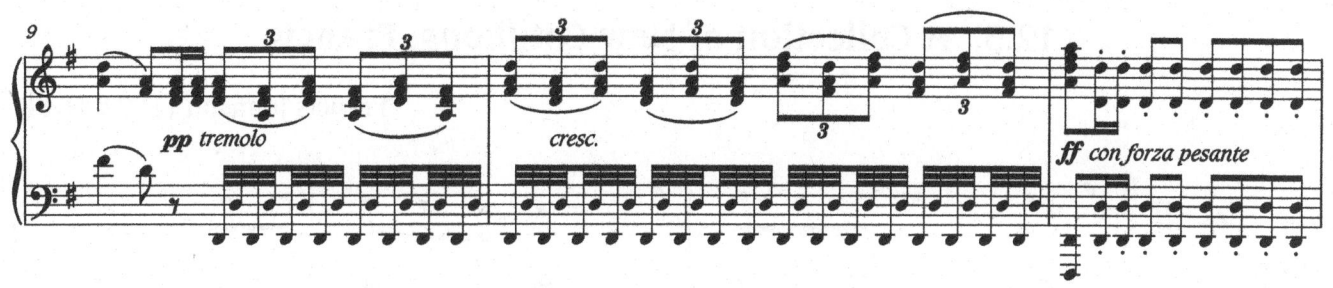

12.3. Trip to Dilington

Ignatius Sancho (c.1729-1780)

12.4. A Collection of New Cotillions: Francis

Francis Johnson (1792-1844)

12.5. A Collection of New Cotillions: Francis

Francis Johnson (1792-1844)

12.6. Sonata No. 5, Op. 16: Adagio

Isabella Leonarda (1620-1704)

12.7. Buvons Lucas

Julie Pinel (fl.1710-1737)

Tonic and Dominant Triads 99

12.8. La disperata

Virginie Morel-du Verger (1799-1870)

13

The Dominant Seventh Chord

This chapter presents the dominant seventh chord in root position and inversions in straightforward examples with either a block chord accompaniment or arpeggiated chords in the lowest voice. All harmonies are diatonic, and the only chords utilized other than the dominant seventh chord are tonic and dominant triads.

ANALYSIS QUESTIONS

1. What is the key of each example?
2. What is the root of each tonic and dominant chord?
3. What is the quality of each tonic and dominant chord?
4. What is the inversion of each tonic and dominant chord?
5. How is the dominant triad different from the dominant seventh chord?
6. What is the function of each dominant seventh chord?
7. How do consecutive inversions of the dominant seventh chord function?
8. How does the leading tone in each dominant seventh chord resolve?
9. How does the chordal seventh in each dominant seventh chord resolve?
10. What embellishing tones occur in each example?

13.1. Ave Sanctissima

Harriet Browne (c.1790-1858)

13.2. En soupirant

María Malibrán (1808-1836)

The Dominant Seventh Chord 103

13.3. Der Mond

Louise Reichardt (1779-1826)

13.4. Wild Flowers

Ida M. Larkins (fl.1905)

13.5. Ombre amene, amiche piante

Isabella Colbran (1785-1845)

13.6. Aurore Pradère

Maud Cuney Hare (1874-1936)

13.7. String Quartet No. 4, Op. 1: Allegro moderato

Joseph Bologne (1745-1799)

13.8. Transports joyeux, Op. 16

Sydney Lambert (1838-1905)

13.9. The Educational Congress March

Anna Gardner Goodwin (1874-1959)

13.10. Deux élégies, Op. 18: Partie!

Teresa Carreño (1853-1917)

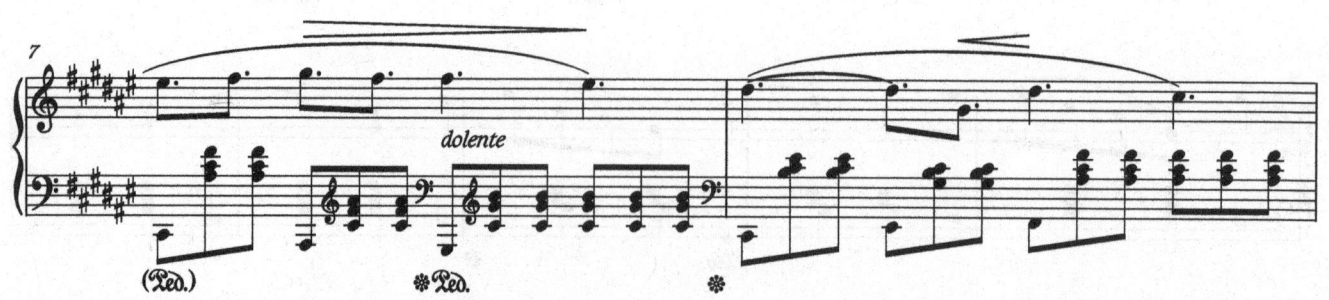

14

The Leading-Tone Triad and Seventh Chord

This chapter presents the leading-tone triad in first inversion and the leading-tone seventh chord in root position and inversions. All harmonies are diatonic, and most examples are primarily composed of tonic and dominant triads and the dominant seventh chord. Predominant harmonies occur briefly in examples 14.3–14.6.

ANALYSIS QUESTIONS

1. What is the key of each example?
2. What is the root of each leading-tone triad and seventh chord?
3. What is the quality of the leading-tone triad?
4. What is the inversion of each leading-tone triad?
5. What is the quality of the leading-tone seventh chord in major keys?
6. What is the quality of the leading-tone seventh chord in minor keys?
7. What is the inversion of each leading-tone seventh chord?
8. How is the leading-tone seventh chord different from the dominant seventh chord?
9. What is the function of each leading-tone triad and seventh chord?

14.1. L'aveu

Hortense de Beauharnais (1783-1837)

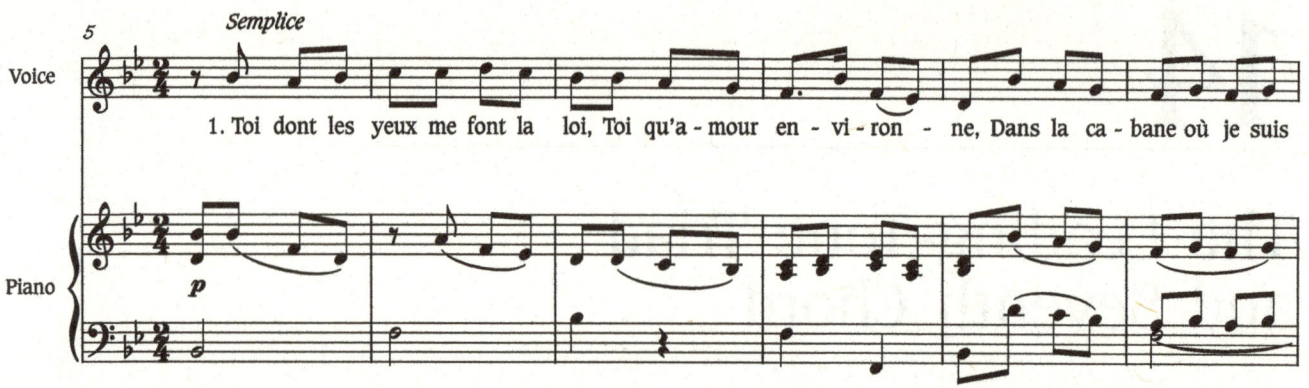

1. Toi dont les yeux me font la loi, Toi qu'a-mour en-vi-ron-ne, Dans la ca-bane où je suis

roi, Viens ré-gner a-vec moi!

14.2. Alerta!

Chiquinha Gonzaga (1847-1935)

14.3. Sonata No. 4, Op. 16: Prestissimo

Isabella Leonarda (1620-1704)

14.4. Violin Sonata No. 5: Aria

Élisabeth Jacquet de la Guerre (1665-1729)

14.5. Les jeunes rêves d'amour

Hortense de Beauharnais (1783–1837)

14.6. Lesson No. 3: Minuetto affetuoso

Elizabeth Turner (1700–1756)

14.7. In the Bottoms: Honey-Humoresque

Robert Nathaniel Dett (1882-1943)

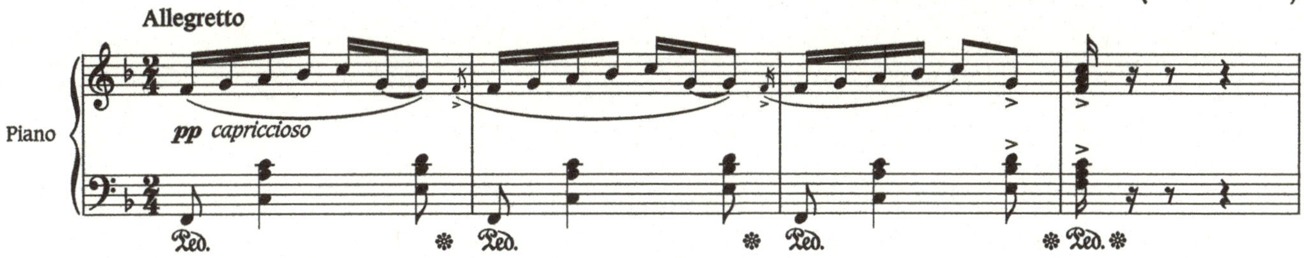
Allegretto
Piano
pp capriccioso
Ped.
Ped.
Ped.
Ped.

14.8. Erinnrung am Bach

Louise Reichardt (1779-1826)

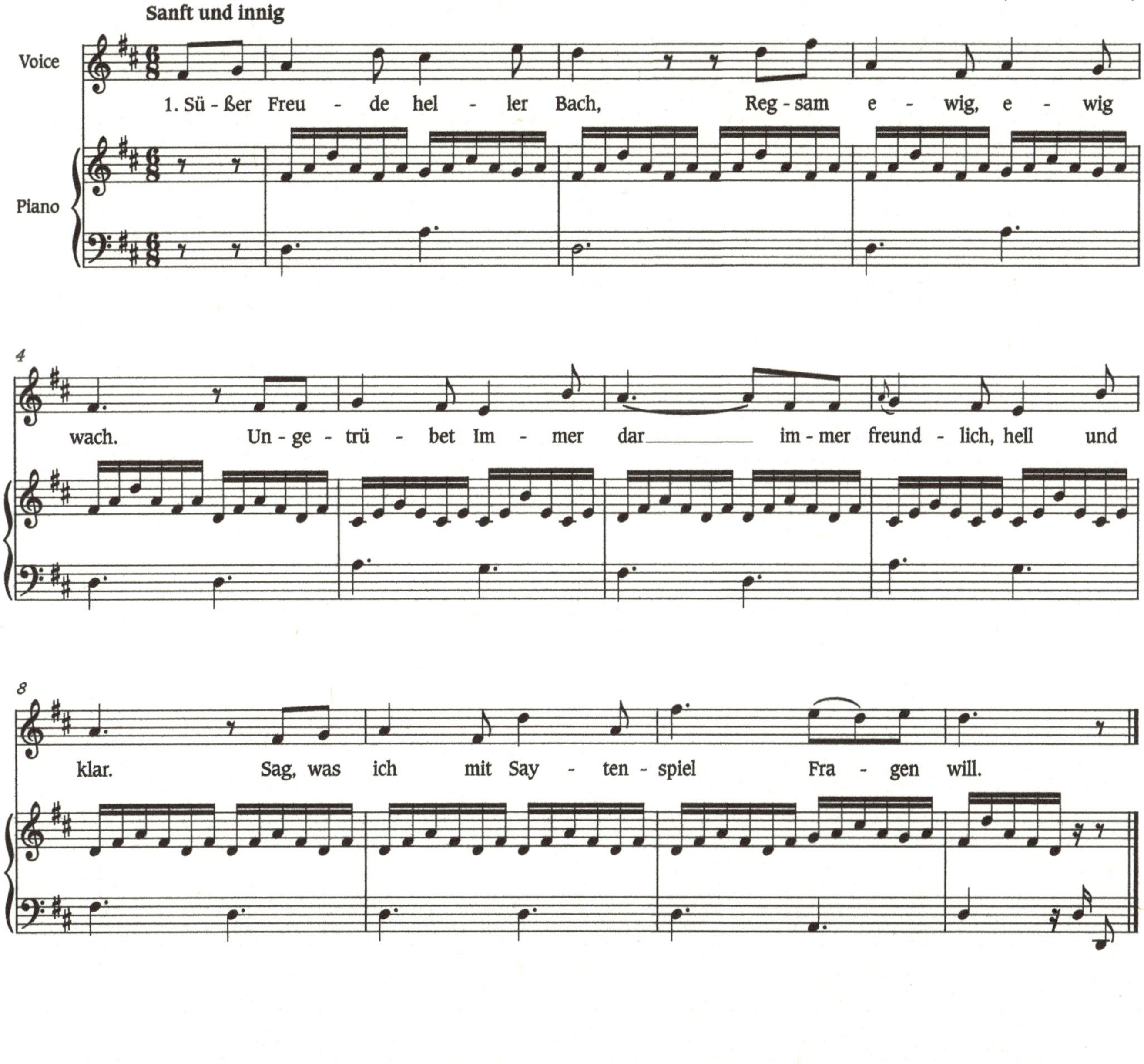
Sanft und innig
Voice
Piano
1. Sü - ßer Freu - de hel - ler Bach, Reg - sam e - wig, e - wig
4
wach. Un - ge - trü - bet Im - mer dar im - mer freund - lich, hell und
8
klar. Sag, was ich mit Say - ten - spiel Fra - gen will.

112   Expanding the Music Theory Canon

15

Predominant Triads and Seventh Chords; the Embellishing Subdominant

This chapter presents various uses of the subdominant and supertonic chords. All harmonies are diatonic, and the examples are primarily composed of the chords covered in chapters 12–14. Examples 15.1–15.11 contain predominant triads, examples 15.12–15.18 illustrate predominant seventh chords, and examples 15.19 and 15.20 demonstrate embellishing subdominants.

ANALYSIS QUESTIONS

1. What is the key of each example?
2. What is the root of each subdominant and supertonic triad?
3. What is the quality of the subdominant triad in major keys?
4. What is the quality of the subdominant triad in minor keys?
5. What is the quality of the supertonic triad in major keys?
6. What is the quality of the supertonic triad in minor keys?
7. What is the inversion of each subdominant and supertonic triad?

8. What is the root of each subdominant and supertonic seventh chord?

9. What is the quality of the subdominant seventh chord in major keys?

10. What is the quality of the subdominant seventh chord in minor keys?

11. What is the quality of the supertonic seventh chord in major keys?

12. What is the quality of the supertonic seventh chord in minor keys?

13. How is the chordal seventh in each subdominant and supertonic seventh chord prepared and resolved?

14. What is the function of each subdominant and supertonic chord in examples 15.1–15.18?

15. What is the function of the subdominant chords in examples 15.19 and 15.20?

15.1. Sonata No. 5, Op. 1: Allegro

Franziska Lebrun (1756-1791)

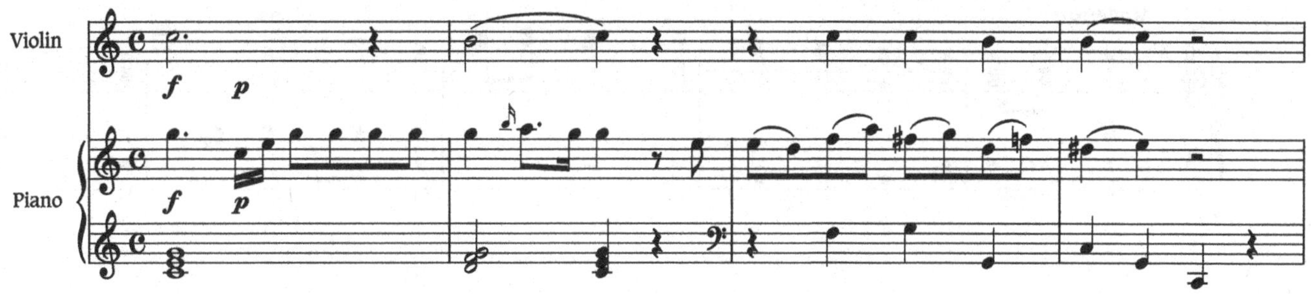
Violin
f p
Piano
f p

15.2. So che un sogno è la speranza

Isabella Colbran (1785-1845)

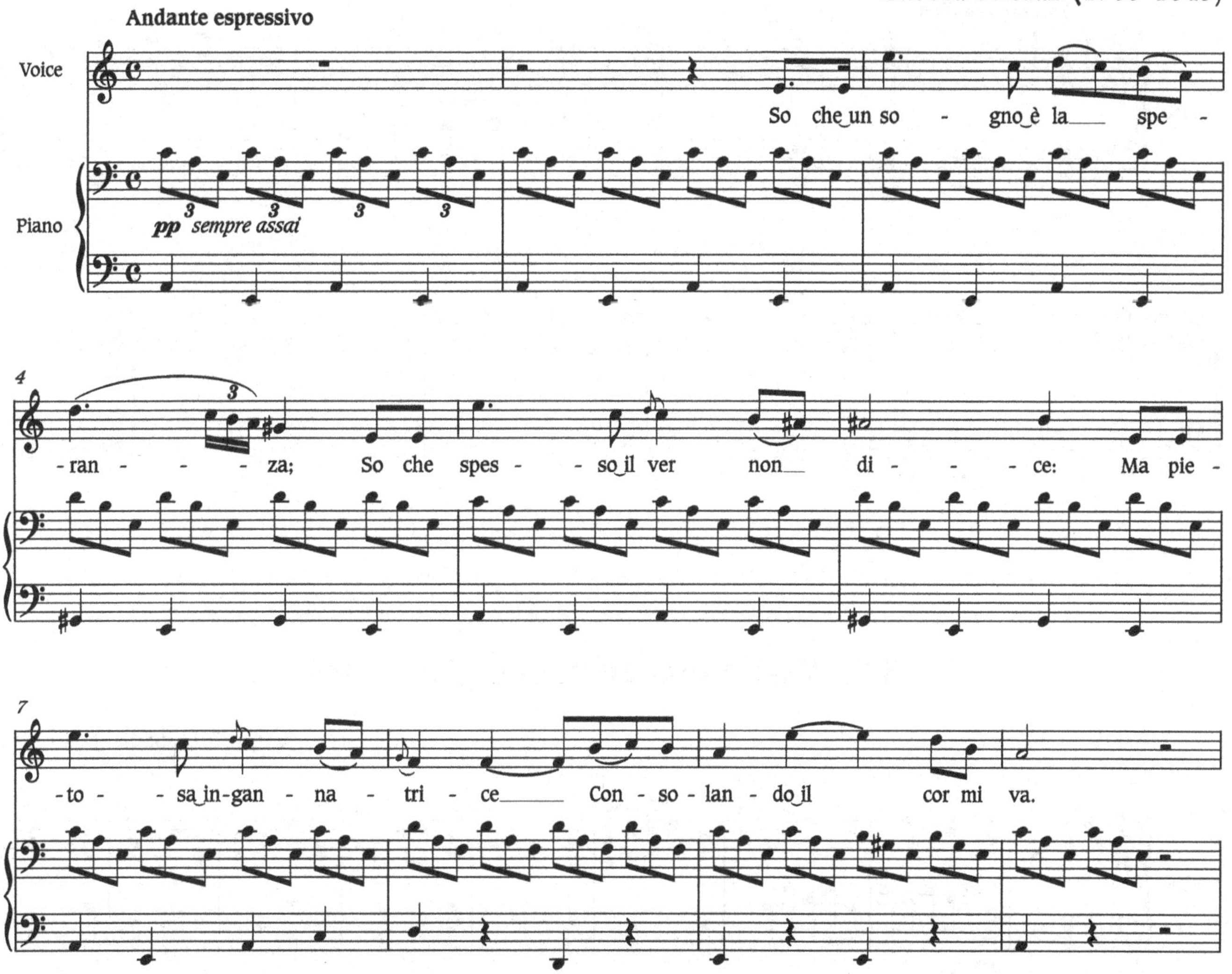
Andante espressivo
Voice
So che un so - gno è la spe -
Piano
pp sempre assai
4
-ran - - - za; So che spes - - so il ver non di - - - ce: Ma pie -
7
-to - - sa in-gan - na - tri - ce Con - so - lan - do il cor mi va.

15.3. Le bon chevalier

Hortense de Beauharnais (1783-1837)

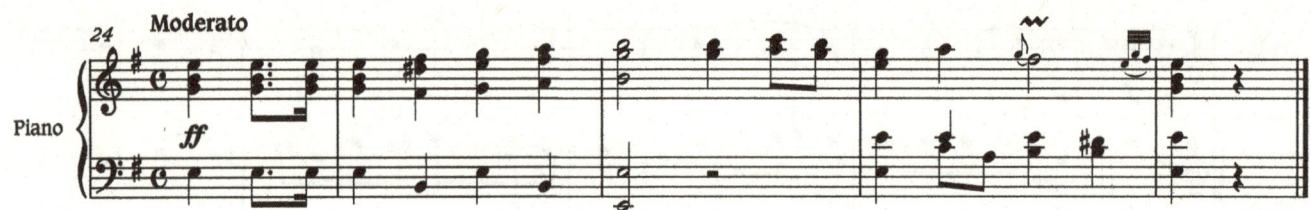

15.4. Arie: All' mein Leben bist du

Josephine Lang (1815-1880)

15.5. Variations on "Beauty in Tears"

Sophia Dussek (b.1775)

15.6. A Collection of New Cotillions: Augustus

Francis Johnson (1792-1844)

15.7. Lesson No. 1: Tambourine

Elizabeth Turner (1700-1756)

15.8. Sonata No. 1, Op. 1a: Allegro

Joseph Bologne (1745-1799)

15.9. Lay de l'exil

Hortense de Beauharnais (1783-1837)

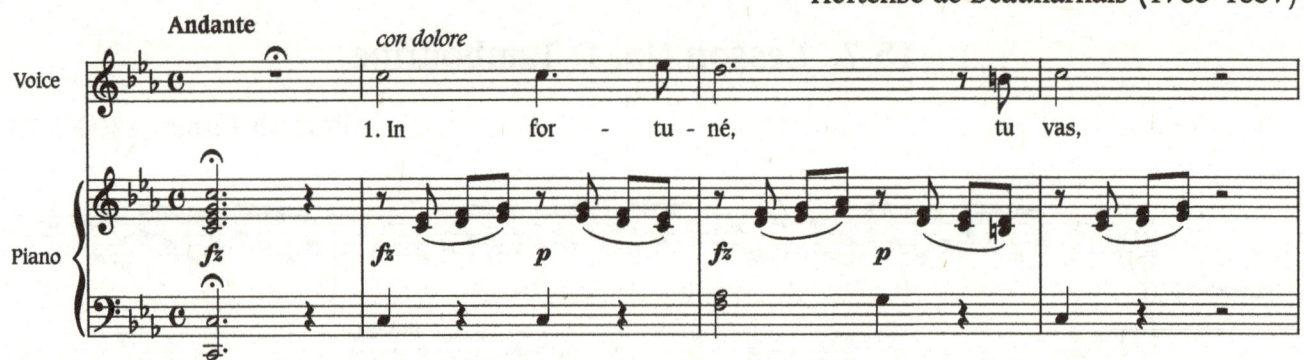

15.10. Lord Dalkeiths Reel

Ignatius Sancho (c.1729-1780)

15.11. String Quartet No. 1, Op. 1: Allegro assai

Joseph Bologne (1745–1799)

15.12. Violin Sonata No. 6: Aria

Élisabeth Jacquet de la Guerre (1665–1729)

15.13. Danse infernale, Op. 46

Josephine Lang (1815–1880)

15.14. Der Winter, Op. 15

Josephine Lang (1815-1880)

1. Der Win - ter ist ein bö - ser Gast, ich fürcht' ihn wie Ge - spen - ster,

15.15. Plus n'aimerai

Hortense de Beauharnais (1783-1837)

15.16. Elegie, Op. 44

Luise Adolpha Le Beau (1850-1927)

15.17. Sonata No. 3, Op. 16: Largo

Isabella Leonarda (1620-1704)

15.18. Sonata No. 7, Op. 16: Largo

Isabella Leonarda (1620-1704)

15.19. Heymdal

Louise Reichardt (1779-1826)

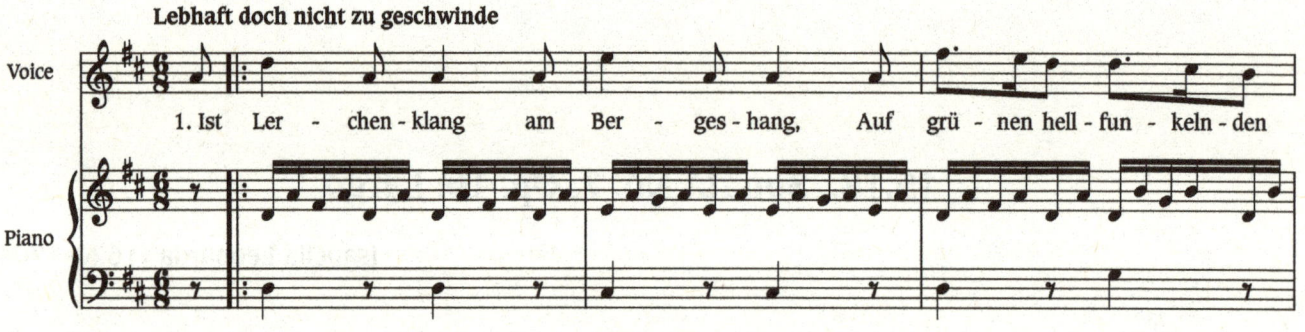

15.20. Aloha Oe

Liliuokalani (1838-1917)

16

Second-Inversion Triads

This chapter presents second-inversion triads with cadential, passing, pedal, and arpeggiating functions. All harmonies are diatonic, and each example is primarily composed of the chords covered in chapters 12–15.

ANALYSIS QUESTIONS

1. What is the key of each example?
2. What is the root of each 6/4 chord?
3. What is the function of each 6/4 chord?
4. Is each 6/4 chord metrically accented or unaccented?
5. Is the root of each cadential 6/4 chord prepared and resolved?
6. How is a 4-3 suspension related to the cadential 6/4 chord's motion to the dominant?

16.1. La sentinelle

Hortense de Beauharnais (1783-1837)

16.2. Spanish Boleros

Sophia Dussek (b.1775)

16.3. Violin Sonata No. 5: Lent

Élisabeth Jacquet de la Guerre (1665-1729)

16.4. Da eben seinem Lauf vollbracht

Maria Theresia von Paradis (1759-1824)

16.5. String Quartet No. 2, Op. 1: Rondeau

Joseph Bologne (1745-1799)

16.6. Three Pictures from Syria: The Desert Patrol

Amanda Aldridge (1866-1956)

16.7. Nuova tarantella

María Malibrán (1808-1836)

16.8. Symphony No. 1, Op. 11: Allegro assai

Joseph Bologne (1745-1799)

16.9. Festmarsch, Op. 31

Josephine Lang (1815-1880)

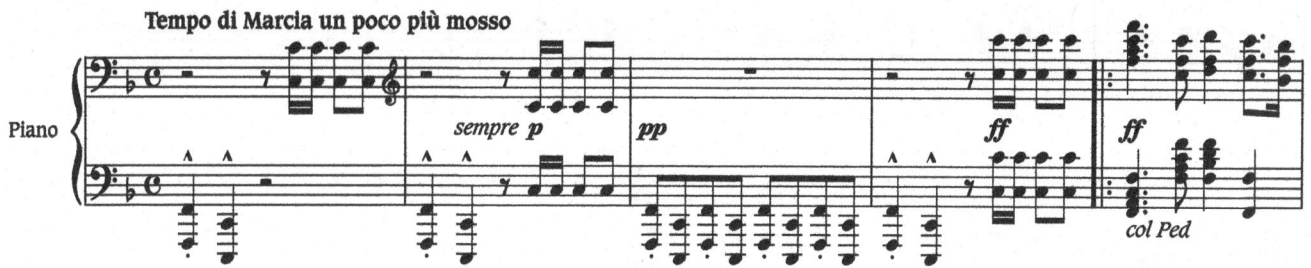

16.10. Dansa das fadas

Chiquinha Gonzaga (1847-1935)

16.11. La chanson du charbonnier

Loïsa Puget (1810-1889)

17

Submediant and Mediant Triads

This chapter presents the submediant and mediant triads in examples that are primarily composed of the diatonic harmonies covered in chapters 12–16. Examples of the mediant triad in minor keys also contain V/III (or the subtonic). For examples of the submediant in deceptive cadences, see chapter 11.

ANALYSIS QUESTIONS

1. What is the key of each example?

2. What is the root of each submediant and mediant chord?

3. What is the quality of the submediant and mediant triads in major keys?

4. What is the quality of the submediant and mediant triads in minor keys?

5. What is the function of each mediant and submediant triad?

6. What tonal center is briefly tonicized in examples 17.6–17.8? How is this tonal center related to the home key of each example?

17.1. Sonata No. 1, Op. 1: Allegro

Franziska Lebrun (1756-1791)

17.2. Romance de Catherine

Julie Candeille (1767-1834)

17.3. Wohl und immer wohl dem Mann

Maria Theresia von Paradis (1759-1824)

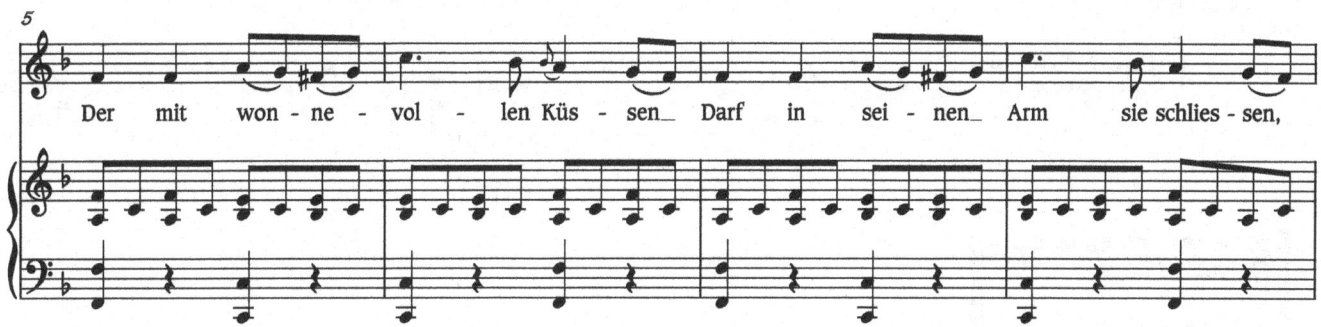

17.4. Terna saudade

Anacleto de Medeiros (1866-1907)

17.5. Sonata No. 11, Op. 16: Allegro

Isabella Leonarda (1620-1704)

17.6. M'entends-tu

Hortense de Beauharnais (1783-1837)

Submediant and Mediant Triads

17.7. Le bon curé patience

Loïsa Puget (1810-1889)

17.8. Violin Sonata, Op. 25: Allegro

Clara Kathleen Rogers (1844-1931)

Submediant and Mediant Triads 137

17.9. Album des enfants, Op. 123: Intermezzo

Cécile Chaminade (1857-1944)

18

Secondary Dominants

This chapter introduces tonicization with secondary dominant and secondary leading-tone triads and seventh chords. All other harmonies in the chapter are diatonic. Examples 18.1–18.6 include secondary dominant triads and seventh chords, while examples 18.7–18.11 contain a combination of secondary dominant and secondary leading-tone triads and seventh chords.

ANALYSIS QUESTIONS

1. What is the key of each example?

2. Is each secondary dominant and secondary leading-tone chord a triad or a seventh chord?

3. What is the quality of each secondary dominant and secondary-leading tone chord?

4. What chord immediately follows each secondary dominant and secondary leading-tone chord? Is this chord the expected resolution? If not, when does a resolution occur?

5. How do the tendency tones in each secondary dominant and secondary leading-tone chord resolve?

6. What is the function of each secondary dominant and secondary leading-tone chord?

18.1. Six morceaux de salon, Op. 26: Un bal en rêve

Teresa Carreño (1853-1917)

18.2. Nach Sevilla

Louise Reichardt (1779-1826)

18.3. String Quartet No. 4, Op. 1: Allegro moderato

Joseph Bologne (1745-1799)

18.4. Carrapatoso

Chiquinha Gonzaga (1847-1935)

18.5. Scherzo, Op. 15

Clara Kathleen Rogers (1844-1931)

18.6. The Clover Blossoms, Op. 10

Clara Kathleen Rogers (1844-1931)

18.7. Nähe des Geliebten, Op. 5

Josephine Lang (1815-1880)

18.8. Violin Sonata No. 1, Op. 10: Allegro con fuoco

Luise Adolpha Le Beau (1850-1927)

18.9. Keyboard Sonata, Op. 3: Ronda alla hornpipe

Cecilia Maria Barthélemon (1767-1859)

18.10. Das Schlüsselloch im Herzen

Emilie Mayer (1812-1883)

18.11. Frühzeitiger Frühling, Op. 6

Josephine Lang (1815-1880)

Secondary Dominants 147

19

Augmented Sixth Chords

This chapter presents Italian, French, and German augmented sixth chords in examples that are primarily composed of diatonic harmonies and secondary dominants.

ANALYSIS QUESTIONS

1. What is the key of each example?
2. What are the scale degrees in an Italian augmented sixth chord?
3. What are the scale degrees in a French augmented sixth chord?
4. What are the scale degrees in a German augmented sixth chord?
5. What chord immediately follows each augmented sixth chord?
6. What is the function of each augmented sixth chord?
7. How does each augmented sixth interval resolve?
8. How is the augmented sixth chord in example 19.8 different from the other augmented sixth chords in this chapter?

19.1. Etude No. 6, Op. 50

Louise Farrenc (1804-1875)

19.2. Das Gärtnerliedchen aus dem Siegwart

Maria Theresia von Paradis (1759-1824)

Augmented Sixth Chords 151

19.3. Irene, Good Night

Gussie Davis (1863-1899)

19.4. Listen to the Lambs

Robert Nathaniel Dett (1882-1943)

Augmented Sixth Chords

19.5. Sonata No. 5, Op. 1: Rondeau

Franziska Lebrun (1756-1791)

19.6. African Dances, Op. 58: No. 1

Samuel Coleridge-Taylor (1875-1912)

19.7. Chicago

Edmond Dédé (c.1827-1901)

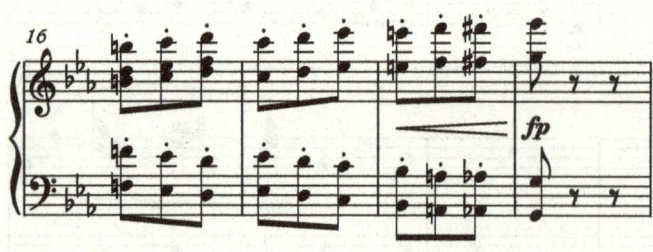

19.8. Ballade, Op. 4

Samuel Coleridge-Taylor (1875-1912)

20

The Neapolitan

This chapter presents examples of the Neapolitan triad in first inversion in excerpts that are primarily composed of diatonic harmonies and secondary dominants.

ANALYSIS QUESTIONS

1. What is the key of each example?
2. What is the quality of each Neapolitan triad?
3. What are the scale degrees in the Neapolitan triad?
4. What is the inversion of each Neapolitan triad?
5. What chord immediately follows each Neapolitan triad?
6. What is the function of each Neapolitan triad?

20.1. Giusto Amor

Louise Reichardt (1779-1826)

20.2. Etude No. 12, Op. 41

Louise Farrenc (1804-1875)

20.3. Wein' aus deine Freude

Josephine Lang (1815-1880)

20.4. La disperata

Virginie Morel-du Verger (1799-1870)

20.5. Deux élégies, Op. 17: Plainte!

Teresa Carreño (1853-1917)

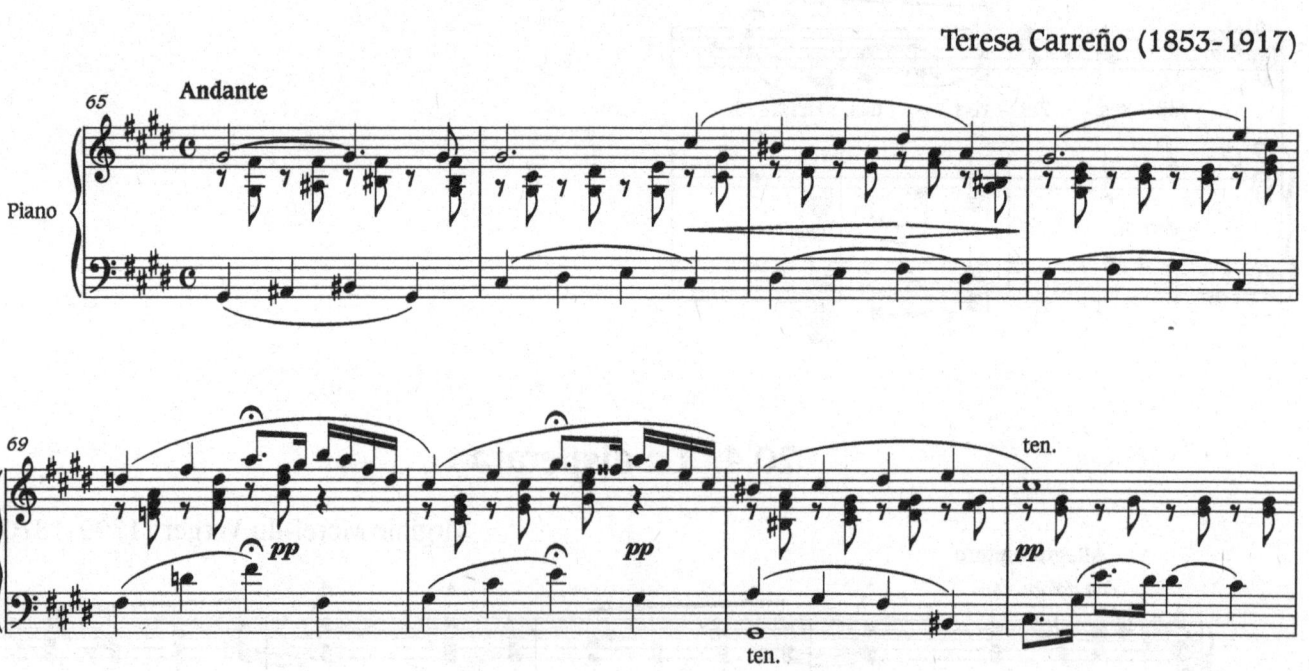

21

Modal Mixture

This chapter presents borrowed supertonic, subdominant, mediant, and submediant chords from the minor mode and a borrowed tonic triad from the major mode. Fluency with secondary dominants, augmented sixth chords, and the Neapolitan is required for most examples in this chapter.

ANALYSIS QUESTIONS

1. What is the key of each example?
2. What is the quality of each borrowed mediant and submediant chord?
3. What is the quality of each borrowed subdominant and supertonic chord?
4. What is the quality of each borrowed tonic triad?
5. How is the Neapolitan different from borrowed chords?
6. How are augmented sixth chords different from borrowed chords?
7. How are secondary dominants different from borrowed chords?
8. What is the function of each borrowed chord?

21.1. Ballade, Op. 4

Samuel Coleridge-Taylor (1875-1912)

Modal Mixture   163

21.2. Deux esquisses italiennes, Op. 33: Venise

Teresa Carreño (1853-1917)

21.3. Trio, Op. 45: Allegro deciso

Louise Farrenc (1804-1875)

Modal Mixture 165

21.4. Three Humoresques, Op. 31: No. 1

Samuel Coleridge-Taylor (1875-1912)

21.5. Chicago

Edmond Dédé (c.1827-1901)

Modal Mixture

21.6. Ai que broma!

Chiquinha Gonzaga (1847-1935)

21.7. Tropical Dance No. 2

Justin Elie (1883–1931)

21.8. Françoise et Tortillard: Duo

Edmond Dédé (c.1827–1901)

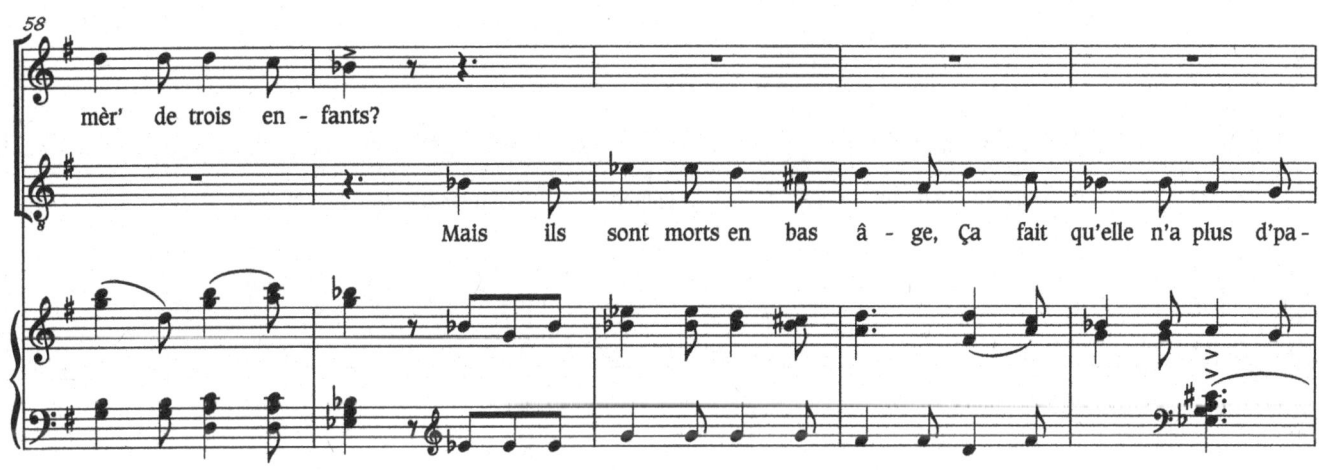

21.9. The Lyre of the Sea Cave

Harriet Browne (1790-1858)

22

Common-Tone Diminished Seventh Chords

This chapter presents common-tone diminished seventh chords as embellishments to the tonic and dominant.

ANALYSIS QUESTIONS

1. What is the key of each example?

2. How is a common-tone diminished seventh chord different from a secondary leading-tone seventh chord?

3. What harmony is being embellished by each common-tone diminished seventh chord?

22.1. Carnival: Pierrette

Amanda Aldridge (1866-1956)

22.2. Le ruisseau, Op. 29

Teresa Carreño (1853-1917)

22.3. Chi

Chiquinha Gonzaga (1847-1935)

22.4. Aurore Pradère

Maud Cuney Hare (1874-1936)

Ya moun qui dit li trop zo-lie, Ya moun qui dit li pas po-lie; Tout ça ya dit, (Sia!)
Some say that she's too pret-ty, quite, some folks they say she's not po-lite; all this they say (Pshaw!)

bin fou bin, C'est li mo ou-lé, c'est li ma pren.
I'm no fool, Oh she's what I want, and her I'll have.

22.5. Vier Lieder für das Pianoforte, Op. 2: No. 4

Fanny Mendelssohn Hensel (1805-1847)

23

Chromatic Mediants

This chapter presents examples of chromatic mediant relationships between consecutive chords and/or tonal centers. Fluency with secondary dominants and modulation is required for each example in this chapter. For additional examples of chromatic mediant relationships in the context of common-tone modulations, see chapter 24.

ANALYSIS QUESTIONS

1. What is the starting key of each example?

2. What is the ending key of each example?

3. Which chords or tonal centers have a chromatic mediant relationship in each example?

4. Which pitch is the common tone between the chords with a chromatic mediant relationship in each example?

23.1. Ninon

Sydney Lambert (1838-1905)

23.2. Valse brillante

Anna Caroline Oury (1808-1880)

Chromatic Mediants — 177

23.3. Zamacueca, Op. 30

José White (1836-1918)

23.4. Trio, Op. 45: Allegro deciso

Louise Farrenc (1804-1875)

24

Diatonic and Chromatic Modulation

This chapter includes examples of diatonic pivot chord modulation and chromatic modulation by common tone, chromatic pivot chord, and enharmonic respelling. Diatonic pivot chord modulations occur in examples 24.1–24.5. These examples are harmonically straightforward and primarily contain chords diatonic to both keys. Examples 24.6–24.12 cover chromatic modulation. These examples require the analyst to also be fluent with modal mixture, secondary dominants, augmented sixth chords, and the Neapolitan. For examples of modulations with sequences, see chapter 25.

ANALYSIS QUESTIONS

1. What is the starting key of each example?

2. What is the ending key of each example?

3. What is the relationship between the starting and ending keys in each example?

4. Is the key that the example modulates to closely related to the home key?

5. What is the best chord to label as the pivot chord in examples 24.1–24.5?

6. What kind of modulation occurs in examples 24.6–24.8? What pitch links the starting and ending keys in each of those examples?

7. What is the name of the relationship between the starting and ending keys in examples 24.6–24.8?

8. What chord connects the starting and ending keys in examples 24.9 and 24.10? Where are these chords borrowed from? What is this type of modulation called?

9. What chord links the starting and ending keys in examples 24.9, 24.11, and 24.12? How do these modulations work? What is this type of modulation called?

Diatonic and Chromatic Modulation

24.1. Etude No. 4, Op. 42

Louise Farrenc (1804-1875)

24.2. Dutchess of Devonshires Reel

Ignatius Sancho (c.1729-1780)

24.3. Que Tircis est charmant

Julie Pinel (fl.1710-1737)

24.4. L'indifférence

María Malibrán (1808-1836)

24.5. Più bella Aurora

Isabella Colbran (1785-1845)

24.6. Trio, Op. 45: Finale

Louise Farrenc (1804-1875)

24.7. Valse, Op. 32

Emilie Mayer (1812-1883)

24.8. Six morceaux de salon, Op. 26: Un bal en rêve

Teresa Carreño (1853-1917)

24.9. Der Neugierige, Op. 10

Emilie Mayer (1812-1883)

24.10. Four Characteristic Waltzes, Op. 22: Valse de la Reine

Samuel Coleridge-Taylor (1875-1912)

24.11. Viennoise, Op. 8

Mélanie Bonis (1858–1937)

24.12. Spring, Op. 20

Clara Kathleen Rogers (1844-1931)

25

Sequences

This chapter presents diatonic and chromatic harmonic sequences. Examples 25.1, 25.2, 25.8, and 25.10 contain only diatonic harmonies; all other examples in the chapter include secondary dominants. Sequences are used to modulate in examples 25.2, 25.4–25.6, 25.9, and 25.12–25.14.

ANALYSIS QUESTIONS

1. What type of sequence(s) occurs in each example?

2. How many chords occur in each sequence model?

3. How many copies of the sequence model occur in each example?

4. How and when does the sequence break?

5. Does the sequence use chromatic chords? If so, what is their quality, and how do they function in relation to the other chords around them?

6. Can you find a repeated melodic pattern in each sequence? If so, does it stay in the same voice, or does it alternate between different voices?

7. Is there a consistent intervallic pattern between the bass and soprano in each model and copy of the sequence?

8. Do the sequences in minor keys use chords from the natural minor, harmonic minor, or melodic minor scale?

9. What is the function of each sequence?

10. How do the preparations and resolutions of each chordal seventh work in sequences with interlocking seventh chords?

11. What are the qualities of chords in each model and copy in examples 25.13 and 25.14? What is the harmonic pattern created by each sequence in those examples?

Sequences 193

25.1. Sonata No. 5, Op. 1: Allegro

Anna Bon (c.1738-after 1769)

25.2. Violin Sonata No. 6: Adagio

Élisabeth Jacquet de la Guerre (1665-1729)

194 Expanding the Music Theory Canon

25.3. Violin Sonata No. 1: Presto

Élisabeth Jacquet de la Guerre (1665-1729)

25.4. Sonata No. 4, Op. 1: Allegro moderato

Anna Bon (c.1738-after 1769)

25.5. Sonata No. 6, Op. 1: Adagio

Anna Bon (c.1738-after 1769)

25.6. Lesson No. 1: Allegro

Elizabeth Turner (1700-1756)

Sequences 197

25.7. Trio, Op. 45: Scherzo

Louise Farrenc (1804-1875)

25.8. Les caractères de l'Amour: Prologue, Air pour les genies

Mademoiselle Duval (1718-after 1775)

25.9. Sonata No. 6, Op. 1: Allegro

Anna Bon (c.1738-after 1769)

25.10. Non scintilate frigide, Op. 11

Isabella Leonarda (1620-1704)

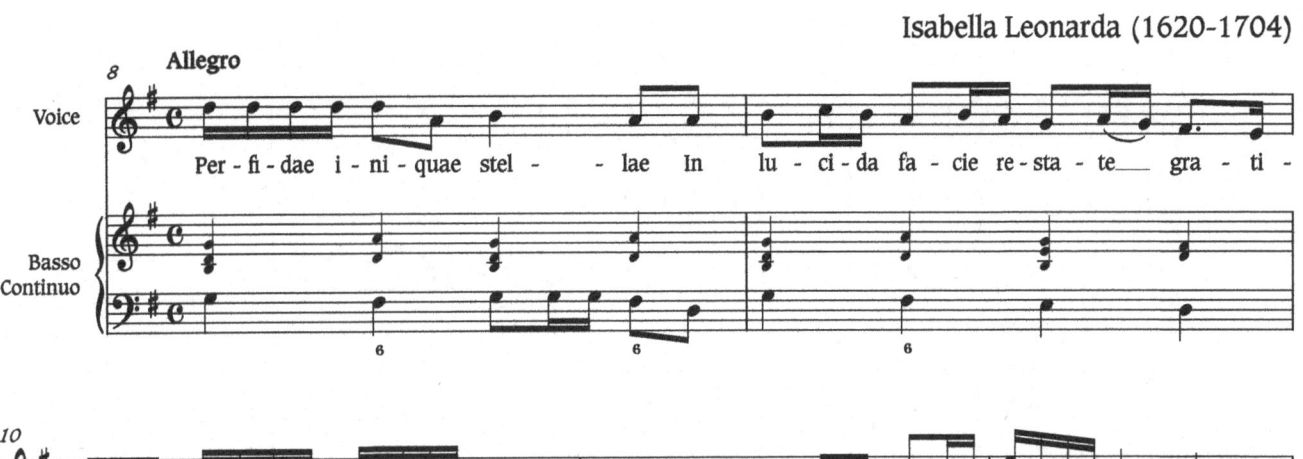

25.11. Sonata No. 2, Op. 1: Largo

Anna Bon (c.1738-after 1769)

25.12. Sonata No. 9, Op. 16: Presto

Isabella Leonarda (1620-1704)

25.13. Erinnerungen an Holland, Op. 33

Leopoldine Blahetka (1809-1885)

25.14. Trio, Op. 45: Allegro deciso

Louise Farrenc (1804-1875)

PART IV
FORMAL STRUCTURES

26

Phrase Structures

This chapter contains periods, sentences, hybrids, double periods, and periods composed of sentences. Fluency with secondary dominants and diatonic pivot chord modulation is required for these examples.

ANALYSIS QUESTIONS

1. What is the starting key of each example?

2. What is the ending key of each example?

3. In examples that modulate, what is the relationship between the starting and ending keys?

4. How many cadences occur in each example?

5. What type(s) of cadence(s) occurs in each example?

6. Divide the phrase structures in examples 26.1–26.9 into four-measure units. What is each four-measure unit called?

7. Where does melodic repetition occur in each phrase?

8. Divide examples 26.10–26.12 into eight-measure and four-measure units. What is each four-measure unit called? What is each eight-measure unit called?

9. What type of phrase structure occurs in each example?

26.1. Da eben seinem Lauf vollbracht

Maria Theresia von Paradis (1759-1824)

26.2. Violin Sonata No. 1, Op. 10: Allegro con fuoco

Luise Adolpha Le Beau (1850-1927)

26.3. Viennoise, Op. 8

Mélanie Bonis (1858-1937)

26.4. Symphony No. 1, Op. 11: Andante

Joseph Bologne (1745-1799)

26.5. Sonata in A Major: Rondo

Marianna Martines (1744-1812)

26.6. Violin Sonata, Op. 25: Allegro

Clara Kathleen Rogers (1844-1931)

26.7. Album des enfants, Op. 123: Gavotte

Cécile Chaminade (1857-1944)

26.8. Méphisto masqué: Introduction

Edmond Dédé (c.1827-1901)

26.9. On the Beautiful Lake Erie

Henry Hart (1839-1915)

26.10. String Quartet No. 1, Op. 1: Rondeau

Joseph Bologne (1745-1799)

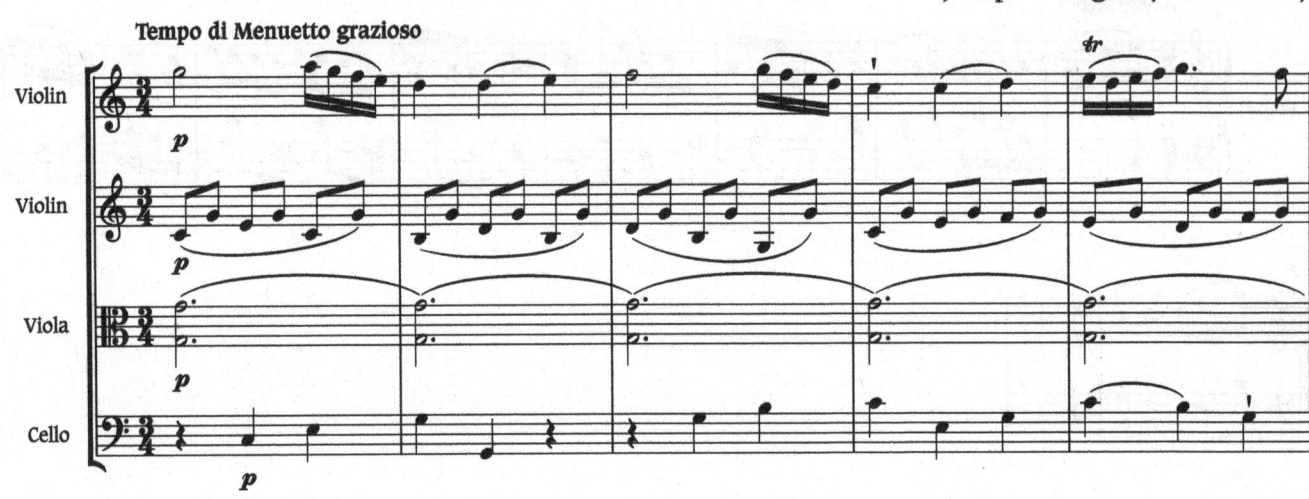

26.11. Trio, Op. 45: Andante

Louise Farrenc (1804-1875)

26.12. Sonata No. 3, Op. 1: Allegro

Maria Frances Parke (1772-1822)

27

Binary Form

This chapter contains simple and rounded binary (or small ternary) forms. Fluency with secondary dominants and diatonic pivot chord modulation is required for these examples. Additionally, example 27.2 contains modal mixture.

ANALYSIS QUESTIONS

1. What is the starting key of each A section?
2. What is the ending key of each A section?
3. If the A section modulates, where does the modulation occur? What is the relationship between the key at the end of the A section and the home key?
4. What is the starting key of each B section?
5. If the B section modulates, where does the modulation occur?
6. Does melodic material from the A section return at the end of the B section?
7. What cadences occur in each example?
8. What phrase structures occur in each example?
9. What is the form of each example?

27.1. Sonata No. 5, Op. 2: Minuet

Jane Savage (c.1752-1824)

27.2. Miaou!! Miaou!!! Op. 238

Eugène Dédé (1867-1919)

27.3. Sonata No. 3, Op. 3: Andantino

Sophia Dussek (b.1775)

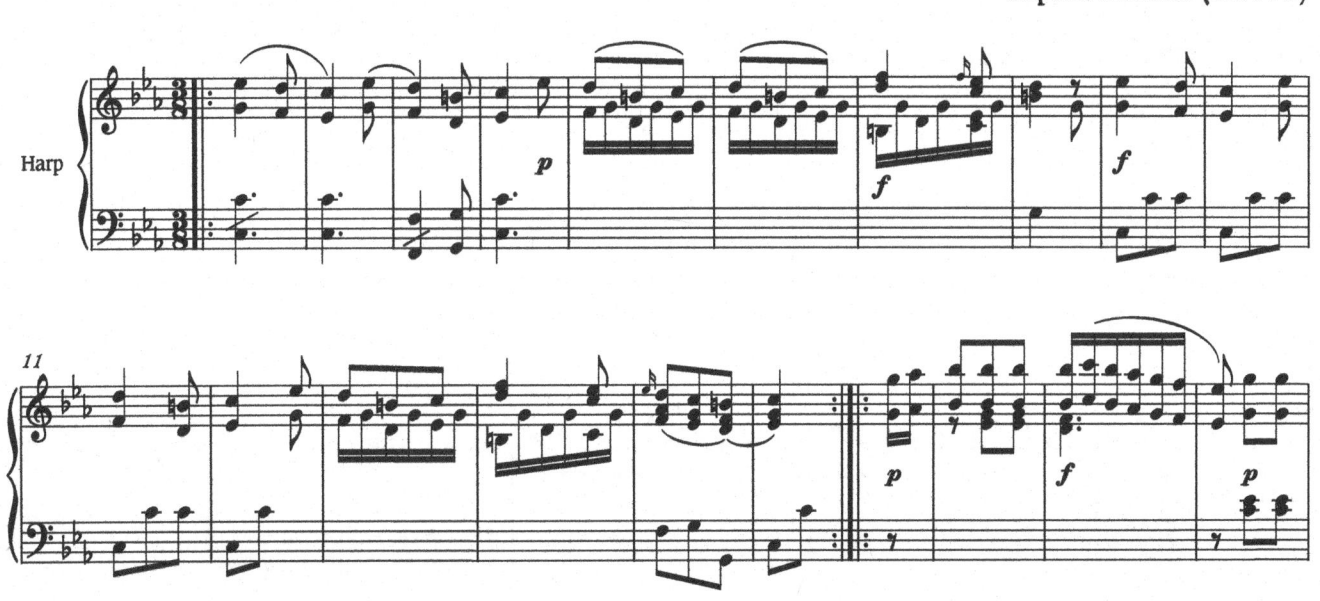

216 Expanding the Music Theory Canon

27.4. Minuet No. 5

Ignatius Sancho (c.1729-1780)

Binary Form 217

27.5. Lesson No. 1: Minuetto

Elizabeth Turner (1700-1756)

28

Sonata Form

This chapter contains three movements in sonata form. Example 28.1 is the most straightforward presentation of the conventional elements of the form, while examples 28.2 and 28.3 each demonstrate slight formal variances. The harmonic language is primarily diatonic, with some secondary dominants and diatonic pivot chord modulations. There are also several augmented sixth chords and occasional occurrences of modal mixture.

ANALYSIS QUESTIONS

1. What is the key at the beginning of the exposition?
2. What is the key at the end of the exposition?
3. What is the relationship between the key at the beginning of the exposition and the key at the end of the exposition?
4. What type of cadence occurs at the end of the main or primary theme?
5. What type of cadence occurs at the end of the transition?
6. Is the transition a modulating transition or a non-modulating transition?
7. How many subordinate or secondary themes occur in the exposition?
8. Is there closing material at the end of the exposition?
9. What tonal centers occur in the development?

10. Are there any sequences in the development?
11. What musical elements from the exposition are utilized in the development?
12. Is there a dominant prolongation before the recapitulation?
13. Where does the development retransition to the recapitulation?
14. How are the tonal centers in the recapitulation different from the tonal centers in the exposition?
15. Are there any significant differences between the recapitulation and the exposition?
16. Does the movement contain a coda?
17. Does the movement contain an introduction?

28.1. Sonata No. 1, Op. 1: Prestissimo

Hélène de Montgeroult (1764-1836)

222 Expanding the Music Theory Canon

Sonata Form 223

Sonata Form 225

Sonata Form 227

28.2. Sonata, Op. 7: Allegro spirito

Maria Hester Park (1760-1813)

Sonata Form 233

234 Expanding the Music Theory Canon

28.3. Sonata No. 1, Op. 1: Allegro

Julie Candeille (1767-1834)

240 Expanding the Music Theory Canon

Sonata Form 241

Sonata Form 243

29

Minuet and Trio

This chapter contains a minuet and trio composed of diatonic harmonies with occasional secondary dominants.

ANALYSIS QUESTIONS

1. What is the form of the minuet?
2. What is the form of the trio?
3. What phrase structures occur in the minuet and the trio?
4. What is the formal structure of the entire movement?

29.1. Sonata No. 2, Op. 1: Menuetto smorfioso and Trio

Maddalena Laura Sirmen (1745-1818)

Minuet and Trio 247

30

Rondo and Sonata-Rondo Forms

This chapter contains examples of ABACA rondos, ABACABA rondos, and a movement in sonata-rondo form. The rondos are harmonically and structurally straightforward and require fluency in secondary dominants, augmented sixth chords, and diatonic pivot chord modulation. The sonata-rondo movement presents some structural analytical challenges and requires fluency with secondary dominants, chromatic mediants, chromatic modulation, diatonic pivot chord modulation, and modal mixture.

ANALYSIS QUESTIONS

1. What is the form of each movement?
2. How many large sections occur in each movement?
3. Is each A section harmonically open or harmonically closed?
4. What phrase structures occur in each example?
5. Are there any smaller binary or ternary formal structures embedded within the larger sections of each rondo?
6. What tonal centers do the B and C sections in each movement modulate to?
7. How are sonata form and rondo form combined in sonata-rondo form?
8. Where does the exposition end in the sonata-rondo form movement?

9. How is the second B section different from the first B section in the sonata-rondo form movement?

10. How does the C section (or development section) in the sonata-rondo form movement differ from the C sections in the other rondos?

11. How is the exposition in the sonata-rondo form movement different from a standard sonata form exposition?

12. What are the differences between the exposition and the recapitulation in the sonata-rondo form movement?

30.1. String Quartet No. 4, Op. 1: Rondeau

Joseph Bologne (1745-1799)

252 Expanding the Music Theory Canon

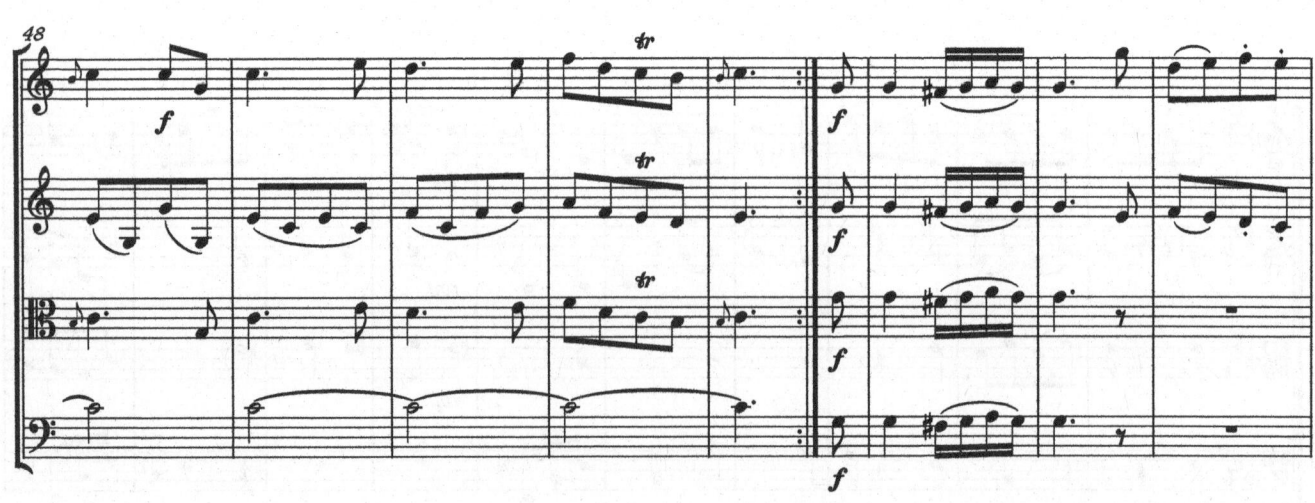

Rondo and Sonata-Rondo Forms 253

30.2. Sonata No. 6, Op. 1: Rondeau

Franziska Lebrun (1756-1791)

Rondo and Sonata-Rondo Forms 255

Rondo and Sonata-Rondo Forms 257

30.3. Sonata No. 3, Op. 2: Rondo

Sophia Dussek (b.1775)

262 Expanding the Music Theory Canon

Rondo and Sonata-Rondo Forms 263

30.4. Sonata No. 3, Op. 1: Rondeau

Franziska Lebrun (1756-1791)

Rondo and Sonata-Rondo Forms 269

Rondo and Sonata-Rondo Forms 271

30.5. Sonata No. 2, Op. 39: Finale

Louise Farrenc (1804-1875)

Rondo and Sonata-Rondo Forms 275

Rondo and Sonata-Rondo Forms 277

278 Expanding the Music Theory Canon

Rondo and Sonata-Rondo Forms

Rondo and Sonata-Rondo Forms 281

Rondo and Sonata-Rondo Forms 285

31

Theme and Variations; Ground Bass

This chapter contains a straightforward Classical theme and variations, a Baroque ground bass, and a late-Romantic ground bass.

ANALYSIS QUESTIONS

1. What is the form of the theme in example 31.1?

2. What phrase structures occur in example 31.1?

3. Does each variation in example 31.1 contain the same harmonic progressions as the theme?

4. What compositional strategies are used to create contrast in each variation of example 31.1?

5. What type of ground bass is used in example 31.2?

6. What compositional strategies are used to create variety in example 31.2?

7. How long is the ground bass in example 31.2?

8. How many times does the ground bass repeat in example 31.2?

9. What compositional strategies are used to create variety in example 31.3?

10. How long is the ground bass in example 31.3?

11. How many times does the ground bass repeat in example 31.3?

12. How is the ground bass in 31.2 different from the ground bass in 31.3?

31.1. Ye Banks & Braes

Sophia Dussek (b.1775)

31.2. Che si può fare, Op. 8

Barbara Strozzi (1619-1677)

Theme and Variations; Ground Bass 293

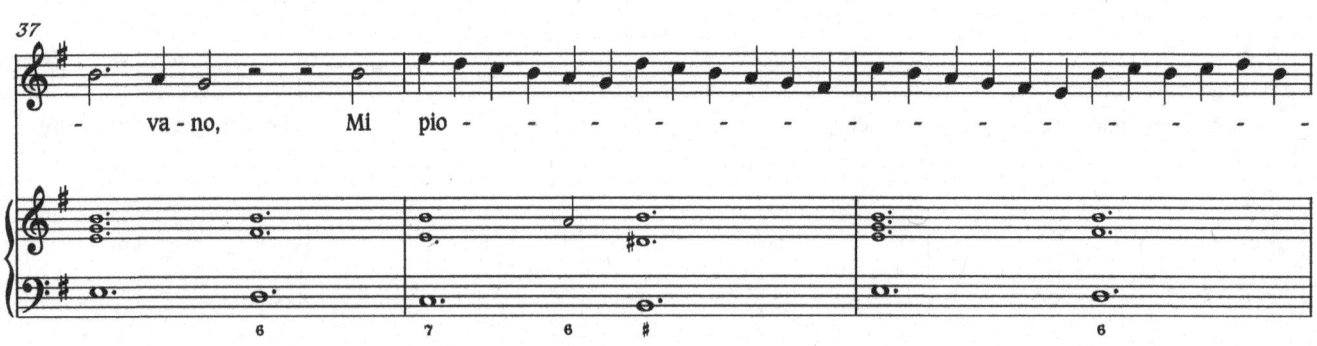

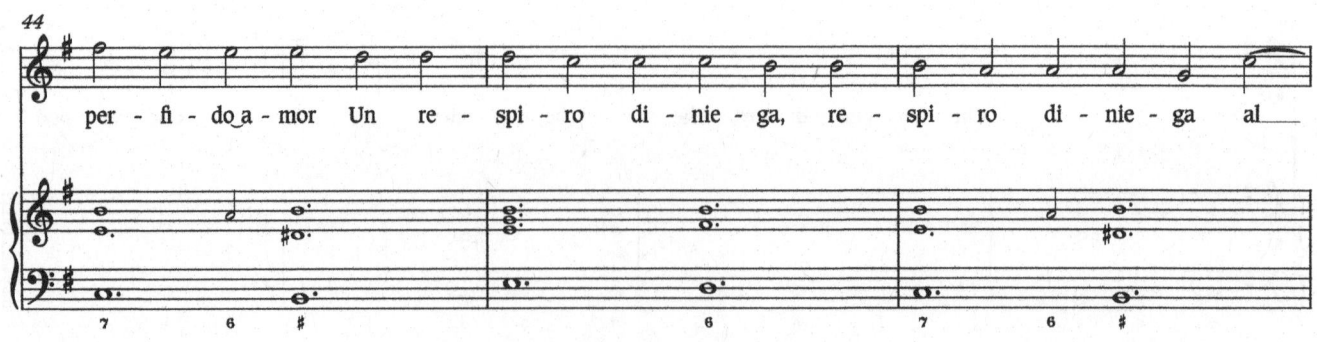

Theme and Variations; Ground Bass 295

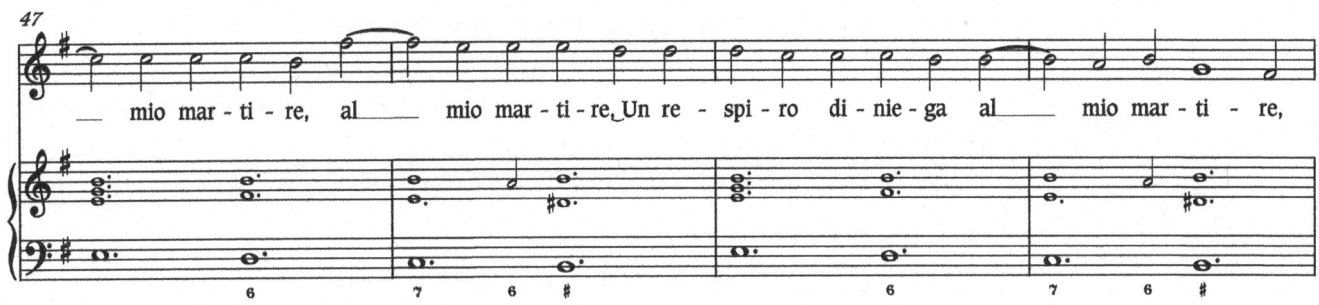

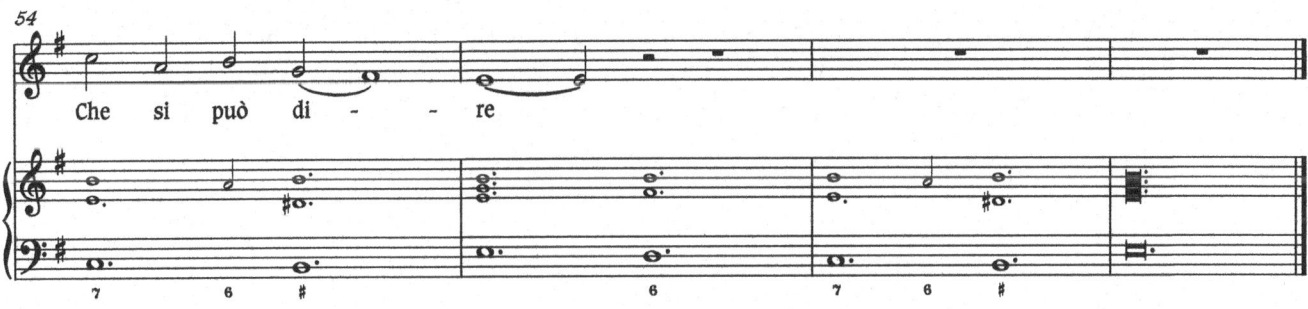

31.3. In the Bottoms: Prelude: Night

Robert Nathaniel Dett (1882-1943)

Theme and Variations; Ground Bass 297

32

Fugue

This chapter contains a nineteenth-century fugue modeled on the fugues in Johann Sebastian Bach's *The Well-Tempered Clavier*.

ANALYSIS QUESTIONS

1. Is the answer real or tonal?

2. Is there a countersubject? If so, how often does the countersubject occur?

3. Where is the end of the exposition?

4. How many episodes are there?

5. What sequences or sequential patterns occur?

6. In what keys do the middle entries of the subject and/or answer occur?

7. Where does melodic inversion occur?

8. Does the composer use stretto, augmentation, diminution, or retrograde? If so, where do those contrapuntal devices occur?

32.1. Fuga No. 1, Op. 16

Clara Schumann (1819-1896)

Fugue 301

33

Large Ternary Form

This chapter contains a slow movement in large (or compound) ternary form that requires fluency in all types of chromatic harmony and modulation.

ANALYSIS QUESTIONS

1. What is the key of the A section?
2. What is the key of the B section?
3. How does the modulation from the A section to the B section work?
4. How does the modulation from the B section to the A' section work?
5. How does the A' section differ from the A section?
6. What phrase structures occur in this movement?
7. Are there any smaller binary or ternary structures embedded within the larger A, B, and A' sections?

33.1. String Quartet in B Minor: Andante

Teresa Carreño (1853-1917)

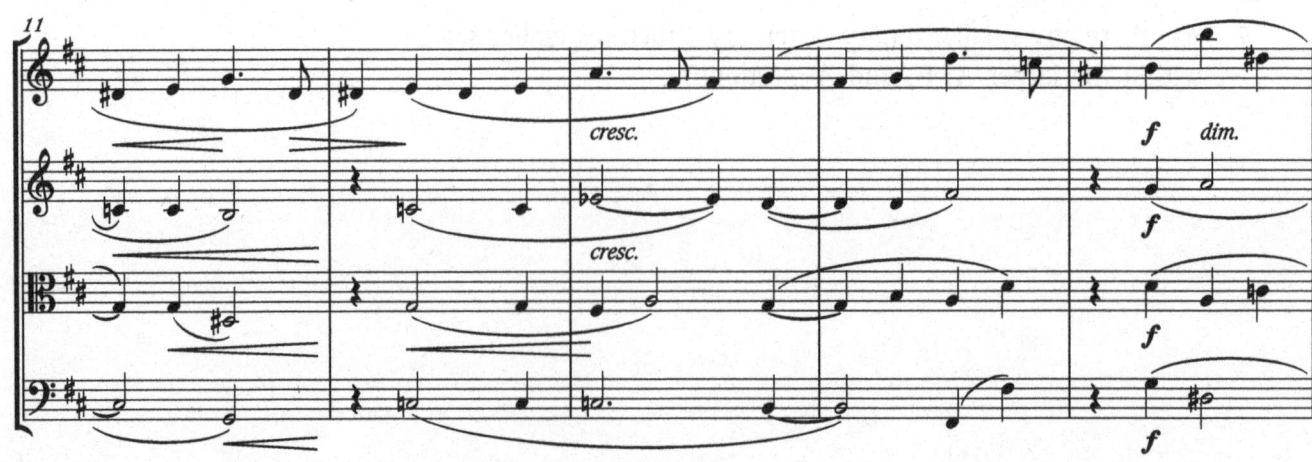

Large Ternary Form 305

Large Ternary Form 307

Large Ternary Form 309

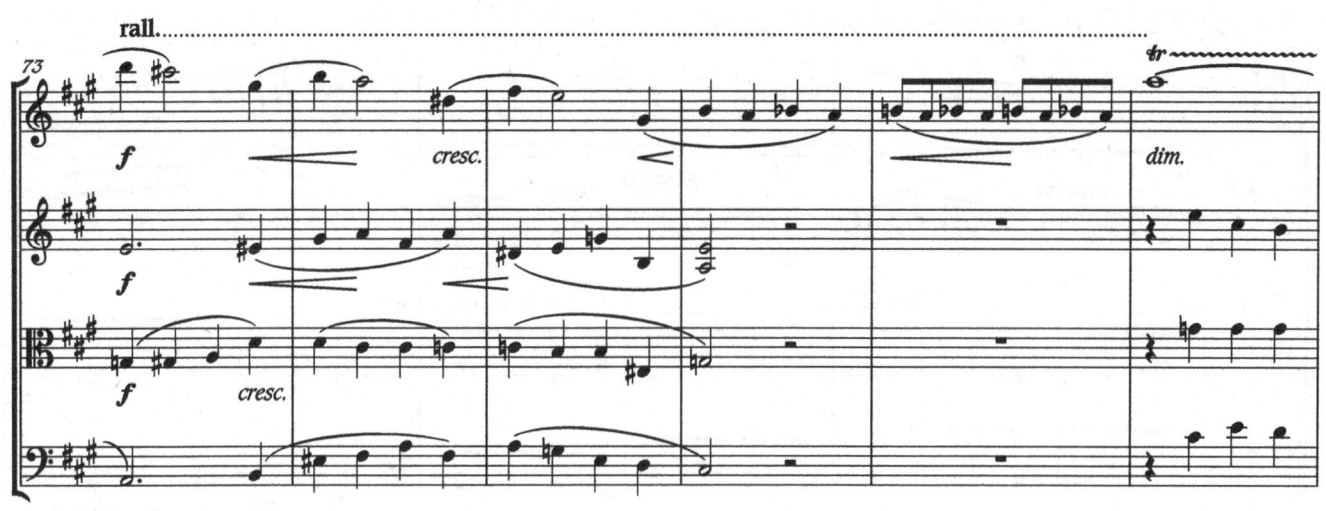

Large Ternary Form 311

COMPOSER BIOGRAPHIES

Figure C.1. Harriett Abrams (c. 1758–1821). "Miss Abrams as Silvia in Cymon, 1778," the Rare Book and Manuscript Library, University of Illinois at Urbana-Champaign. Public domain.

Harriett Abrams (c. 1758–1821) was an English actress, soprano, and composer of Jewish descent. She made her stage debut in 1775 at Drury Lane in London, where she continued to sing and act for the next five seasons. Abrams then enjoyed a successful career as a soloist at prestigious London concerts, including the Handel Commemoration festivals, the Academy of Ancient Music, and the Concerts of Antient Music. Charles Burney declared in 1784 that her voice was "sweet and of a good quality" and asserted that she sang with "considerable taste and expression." In the next decade, Abrams collaborated with Franz Joseph Haydn and members of her family in annual benefit concerts, often premiering her own works. In addition to her four books of English, Italian, and Scottish songs, several individual songs by Abrams were printed in contemporaneous publications in the United States.

Figure C.2. Amanda Ira Aldridge (1866–1956). The A. M. E. Review, July 1884, Library of Congress, Rare Book and Special Collections Division. Public domain.

Amanda Ira Aldridge (1866–1956) was an English contralto, teacher, and composer who published under the pseudonym Montague Ring. Two years after her 1881 singing debut at the Crystal Palace in London, Aldridge won a competitive scholarship to study with Jenny Lind at the Royal College of Music. Aldridge then performed as a recitalist for several decades, garnering numerous favorable reviews. The London *Times* wrote in June 1905, for example, "Miss Aldridge's style is excellent, her voice warm and mellow, and her intelligence far beyond dispute; the combination may well serve to explain the measure of her success." After her throat was damaged from severe laryngitis, Aldridge focused on teaching and composing. In particular, she was known for her mentorship of the next generation of Black singers, including Marian Anderson and Paul Robeson. She was a revered pedagogue in vocal production and elocution and continued to teach well into her eighties. Much of Aldridge's compositional output was popular parlor music for voice and piano, which was printed by major London publishing houses.

Figure C.3. Cecilia Maria Barthélemon (1767–1859). Cover of Barthélemon's Keyboard Sonata, Op. 3. Public Domain.

Cecilia Maria Barthélemon (1767–1859) was an English singer, pianist, organist, and composer who was born into a family of professional musicians. On her parents' 1776–1777 continental tour, she sang for King Ferdinand IV of Naples and Queen Marie-Antoinette of France. She then performed at her mother's 1778 benefit concert in London and continued to sing and play the piano in recitals with her parents. Barthélemon was friends with Franz Joseph Haydn, to whom she dedicated her Keyboard Sonata, Op. 3. Her compositions include a vocal piece and four collections of keyboard sonatas, some with violin or flute accompaniment. More than three hundred people subscribed to her first book of sonatas, including prominent English musicians and social elites. There is no documentation of Barthélemon's musical career after her marriage in 1797.

Figure C.4. Marion Bauer (1882–1955); George Maillard Kesslere, c. 1920. *The Musical Leader*, 1920. Public domain.

Marion Bauer (1882–1955) was an American composer, educator, scholar, and author who championed the works of young composers. She was a founding member and/or leader in every major composers' organization of her time, including the International Society for Contemporary Music, the American Music Guild, the Society of American Women Composers, the American Composers Alliance, the Society for the Publication of American Music, and the League of Composers. Bauer taught music history and composition at New York University for twenty-five years and was renowned as a lecturer who could appeal to both amateurs and experts. She was also a music critic and published numerous books and articles. Bauer's compositional output includes at least 160 solo piano pieces, art songs, choral works, chamber music, and orchestral works. Many of her pieces were performed by prestigious ensembles.

Figure C.5. Amy Beach (1867–1944); Elmer Chickering, n.d. George Grantham Bain Collection, Library of Congress, Prints and Photographs Division, LC-USZ62-65092. Public domain.

Amy Beach (1867–1944) was a composer, a pianist, and the first American woman to have a symphony performed by a major orchestra. A child prodigy, Beach was reported to be able to sing forty tunes at age one; she mentally composed her first piano pieces at the age of four; and she could easily play by ear as a young child. Beach made her debut as a pianist in 1883 with the Boston Symphony Orchestra. Out of respect for her husband's request that she cease performing publicly, Beach focused primarily on composition after her marriage in 1885. She spent the next ten years studying the works of historical composers and translating music theory treatises to teach herself counterpoint, form, harmony, and orchestration. Beach was able to write entire large-scale works in just a few days, most of which were published by Arthur P. Schmidt. After being widowed in 1910, Beach toured Europe and the United States to establish herself as both a composer and a performer. She spent the rest of her life composing, performing, and actively promoting her own works.

Figure C.6. Hortense de Beauharnais (1783–1837); Anne-Louis Girodet-Trioson, c. 1805–1809, Rijksmuseum, Amsterdam.

Hortense de Beauharnais (1783–1837) was a French singer, pianist, and noblewoman who composed 124 romances for voice and piano. It is likely that she wrote the melodies for her songs and then collaboratively created the accompaniments with the assistance of professional court musicians. François-Joseph Fétis praised Hortense's melodies in his 1869 *Biographie Universelle des Musiciens*, and Antoine Vialon published her complete works. At least one of her songs inspired the publication of sets of piano variations by Johann Nepomuk Hummel and Franz Schubert. Hortense was the stepdaughter of Napoleon Bonaparte, and she was briefly married to his brother Louis. During this marriage, Hortense was the Queen of Holland. After separating from her husband and returning to France, she became the Duchess of Saint-Leu.

Figure C.7. Leopoldine Blahetka (1809–1885). Österreichische Nationalbibliothek Bildarchiv und Grafiksammlung. Public domain.

Leopoldine Blahetka (1809–1885) was an Austrian pianist, composer, and teacher whose extensive sixty-year career had a substantial impact on the public's perception of professional women pianists. Ludwig van Beethoven was particularly invested in her musical development and arranged for her to study with Joseph Czerny. In 1820, Blahetka was the soloist for Beethoven's Piano Concerto No. 2, Op. 19, and she was praised for her precision, technique, touch, and expressiveness. As early as 1823 she was playing her own compositions in recitals across Europe. Her compositional output includes sixty-four solo piano, chamber, orchestral, vocal, and stage works.

Figure C.8. Joseph Bologne (1745–1799); Mather Brown, 1788. Beaux-Arts de Paris, Dist. RMN-Grand Palais/Art Resource, NY. Public domain.

Joseph Bologne (1745–1799) was a violinist, fencer, conductor, and composer born to an enslaved Black Guadeloupean woman and her French enslaver. Bologne's father acknowledged Joseph as his son and relocated the family to France for Joseph to be educated. Bologne excelled greatly in all his musical and athletic pursuits, and he earned the title Chevalier de Saint-Georges at age nineteen. In addition to composing numerous large-scale orchestral, chamber, and stage works, Bologne was a renowned violin virtuoso and conductor. He founded the Concert de la Loge Olympique, and under his direction the Concert des Amateurs was regarded as one of the best orchestras in Western Europe. In 1776, a group of Parisian singers petitioned the Queen to block Bologne's appointment as music director to the Paris Opera because of his race. Such events increased Bologne's hope for true equality for all people, thereby compelling him to join the French Revolution and serve as a colonel in the Légion des Américains et du Midi.

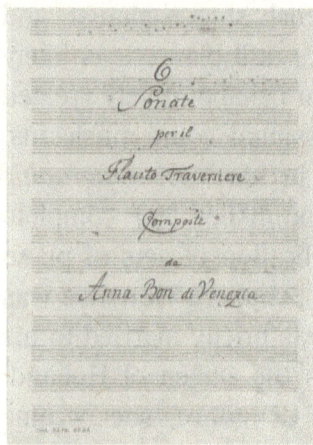

Figure C.9. Anna Bon (c. 1738–after 1769). Cover of Bon's *6 Sonate per il Flauto Traversiere*. Public domain.

Anna Bon (c. 1738–after 1769) was an Italian harpsichordist and composer born into a family of professional court musicians and artists. At the age of four, she was admitted to the Venetian Ospedale della Pietà as a private music student. The specific details of her professional life are uncertain, but she likely remained at the Pietà until she joined her parents at the Brandenburg court as a teenager. She was performing with her family in Pressburg in 1759, and her family was hired by the Esterházy court of Prince Nicolaus of Eisenstadt in 1762. Bon remained in that position until at least 1765. Her three books of harpsichord and flute sonatas were published by the Schmid firm in Nuremberg.

Figure C.10. Mélanie Bonis (1858–1937); Charles-Auguste Corbineau, 1877. Association Mel Bonis. Public domain.

Mélanie Bonis (1858–1937) was a French organist, pianist, and composer who published under the masculine pseudonym Mel Bonis. Her parents were not supportive of her musical studies, and Bonis was mostly self-taught until a family friend advocated for her to have formal lessons. Bonis later studied at the Paris Conservatory with César Franck and Ernest Guiraud from 1876 until 1881, when her parents forced her to withdraw and marry. She began composing in 1894, ultimately writing more than three hundred piano, choral, organ, vocal, and orchestral works.

Figure C.11. Nadia Boulanger (1887–1979); Bain News Service, 1925. George Grantham Bain Collection, Library of Congress, Prints and Photographs Division, LC-USZ62-85142. Public domain.

Nadia Boulanger (1887–1979) was a French composer, pianist, organist, conductor, and one of the most revered teachers of the twentieth century. She won second place in the Prix de Rome in 1908, thereby launching her compositional career. Boulanger's publications include vocal, chamber, and orchestral works. A frequent organ and piano soloist, she toured the United States in 1925 to premiere Aaron Copland's symphony for organ and orchestra. Boulanger was also one of the first prominent women orchestral conductors, and she conducted the London Philharmonic, the Boston Symphony Orchestra, the Philadelphia Orchestra, and the New York Philharmonic. Much of her career was dedicated to teaching, and she held appointments at the Conservatoire Femina-Musica, the École Normale de Musique, and the Paris Conservatory. She was a founding member and director of the American Conservatory at Fontainebleau.

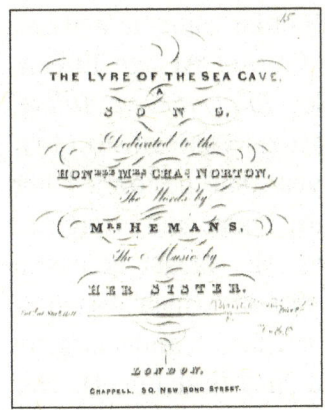

Figure C.12. Harriet Browne (c. 1790–1858). Cover of Browne's *The Lyre of the Sea Cave*. Public domain.

Harriet Browne (c. 1790–1858) was an English composer of popular songs and duets, many of which utilized the texts of her sister Felicia Hemans, a well-known poet. Browne's music was well-received in both the United States and England, and many of her songs were extensively reprinted. For example, Browne's "Tyrolese Evening Hymn" appeared in more than sixty editions, and "The Breaking Waves Dash High" had at least forty-six printings. Additionally, a number of her works were arranged for school choirs and quartets. In 1839, Browne edited her sister's complete works into seven volumes and published them with a memoir.

Figure C.13. Harry Thacker Burleigh (1866–1949); Lily Hardy Hammond, 1922. Schomburg Center for Research in Black Culture, Jean Blackwell Hutson Research and Reference Division, New York Public Library. Public domain.

Harry Thacker Burleigh (1866–1949) was an American singer, composer, arranger, and music editor who is credited with introducing Antonin Dvořák to spirituals and plantation songs, which Burleigh learned from his formerly enslaved grandfather. For more than fifty years, Burleigh was the baritone soloist at St. George's Protestant Episcopal Church in New York. His art songs were regarded as among the best of his time, although his primary legacy today is considered to be his arrangements of spirituals. These arrangements were crafted during the fifteen years Burleigh sang for Booker T. Washington's fundraising events, and the pieces continue to be performed extensively by prestigious choirs and soloists. As the staff editor of the New York office of G. Ricordi from 1913 until 1941, Burleigh facilitated the publication of works by other Black composers. The *New York Herald Tribune* wrote in his obituary that Burleigh's "warm, instinctive humanity, reflected in his voice, brought him friends of every class, race, and creed. His long life was as happy and triumphant as the spirituals he loved to sing."

Figure C.14. Francesca Caccini (1587–after 1641). Cover of Caccini's *Il primo libro delle musiche*. Public domain.

Francesca Caccini (1587–after 1641) was an Italian singer, teacher, and composer employed as a court musician by the Medici family. She ultimately became the highest-paid musician on the Medici payroll and is widely regarded as the first Western European woman to compose a fully-plotted and staged musical-dramatic work. In addition to composing and performing, Caccini was charged with teaching noblewomen, and her 1618 collection of thirty-six solo songs and duets was likely intended to be pedagogical. Caccini was highly educated and dedicated to the lifelong pursuits of learning and honing her craft. In a 1617 letter to her colleague Michelangelo Buonarroti, she wrote, "I would lose my life before my desire to study and the affection I have always had for virtue, because this is worth more than any treasure or grandeur."

Figure C.15. Julie Candeille (1767–1834); Adélaïde Labille-Guiard, 1791. Private collection. Wikimedia, public domain.

Julie Candeille (1767–1834) was a composer, librettist, singer, actress, instrumentalist, and writer active in revolutionary France. At age fifteen, she sang the title role in Christoph Willibald Gluck's *Iphigénie en Aulide*, and she subsequently played a piano concerto by Muzio Clementi to great acclaim at the Concert Spirituel in Paris. The next year, she performed her own piano concerto. Candeille also composed dramatic music and wrote her own plays, for which she often acted the title roles. Her most successful stage work was the 1792 *Catherine, ou La belle fermière*, which was performed more than 150 times during the next three decades. Candeille gave piano lessons and published essays, memoirs, and historical novels. Her musical compositions include stage works, a piano concerto, vocal music, and solo piano works.

Figure C.16. Teresa Carreño (1853–1917); the *New York Musical Courier*, December 2, 1896. Rebekah Crawford Collection, Library of Congress, Music Division, Album of Musicians. Public domain.

Teresa Carreño (1853–1917) was a Venezuelan composer, impresario, singer, and teacher who was one of the first women pianists to tour the United States. Known as the "Valkyrie of the piano," she began her extraordinary performance career as a young child in Caracas and made her New York debut at age eight. Two years later, Abraham Lincoln invited her to perform at the White House. In the coming decades, she toured extensively in the United States, Europe, the Caribbean, and Venezuela. Students often traveled to her summer residence to study for extended periods of time, and women composers and pianists looked up to her as a role model. Nearly all of Carreño's approximately eighty compositions, which include virtuosic works for solo piano, a string quartet, and a string orchestra serenade, were printed by esteemed publishing houses. Both Amy Beach and Edward MacDowell dedicated piano concertos to her.

Figure C.17. Maddalena Casulana (c. 1544–c. 1590). Cover of Casulana's *Il secondo libro de madrigali*. Public domain.

Maddalena Casulana (c. 1544–c. 1590) was an Italian composer, lutenist, and singer who was the first known woman to publish a book of madrigals. By the end of her career, she had written three books of madrigals, each dedicated to a different patron. The introduction to her 1568 collection asserted that the work was "to show the world (as much as I can in this profession of music) the foolish error of men who so greatly believe themselves to be the masters of high intellectual gifts that [these gifts] cannot, it seems to them, be equally common among women." Casulana also defied cultural expectations by confidently singing her own works in public, a provocative act for which she received both high praise and vehement criticism.

Figure C.18. Cécile Chaminade (1857–1944). Anne Shaw Faulkner, *What We Hear in Music*, Victor Talking Machine Company, 1913. Public domain.

Cécile Chaminade (1857–1944) was a French composer and pianist whose approximately four hundred compositions were published during her lifetime. Even though her father prohibited her from officially enrolling as a student at the Paris Conservatory, Chaminade studied privately and eventually became the first woman composer admitted to the Légion d'Honneur in 1913. Her character pieces and *mélodies* were quite popular, and she promoted sales of her works through extensive concert tours in Europe and the United States. Critics were polarized in their receptions of Chaminade's music. Her lyrical character pieces were deemed by some to be too feminine, while her pieces based on thematic development were considered too masculine. Between 1901 and 1914, Chaminade made several recordings on piano rolls, and Aeolian produced additional recordings of her music utilizing advanced technologies after World War I. Her compositional output includes solo piano pieces, mélodies, orchestral works, and chamber music.

Figure C.19. Isabella Colbran (1785–1845); Johann Heinrich Schmidt, 1817. Museo Teatrale alla Scala, Milan. Public domain.

Isabella Colbran (1785–1845) was a Spanish soprano and composer acclaimed for her dramatic stage presence and vocal range of nearly three octaves. She made her concert debut in Paris in 1801 and her opera debut in Spain in 1806. Known for her commanding portrayals of tragic characters, she captivated audiences for more than a decade in Milan, Naples, Venice, and Vienna. The Rossinian operatic roles she created include the title roles of Elisabetta, Regina d'Inghilterra, Armida, Ermione, and Zelmira. She also premiered Desdemona in *Otello*, Elcia in *Mosè in Egitto*, Zoraide in *Ricciardo e Zoraide*, Elena in *La donna del lago*, and Anna in *Maometto II*. Colbran composed four volumes of songs that were dedicated to the Empress of Russia, Girolamo Crescentini, and the Queen of Spain.

Figure C.20. Samuel Coleridge-Taylor (1875–1912). Library of Congress, Prints and Photographs Division, LC-USZ62-122324. Public domain.

Samuel Coleridge-Taylor (1875–1912) was an English composer, conductor, and educator who wrote more than eighty piano, chamber, orchestral, vocal, and stage works. In addition to composing, he conducted the Handel Society of London and was the Professor of Composition at the Guildhall School of Music and the Trinity College of Music. Coleridge-Taylor's musical career and activism had a wide-reaching impact across Europe and the United States. His compositions inspired the formation of the Coleridge-Taylor Choral Society, a group of two hundred Black singers in Washington, DC. In 1904, he conducted the Choral Society and the United States Marine Band in a program of his own works, and an elementary school in Baltimore,

Maryland, is named after him. Coleridge-Taylor advocated strongly for Black rights and wrote a number of works inspired by his African heritage. After his premature death from pneumonia, crowds lined the streets of Croydon for three and a half miles to witness his funeral procession.

Gussie Davis (1863–1899) was an American composer who became one of the most sought-after songwriters of Tin Pan Alley and was the first Black American to win international acclaim for his ballads. After working as a janitor at the Nelson Musical College in Cincinnati, Ohio, he relocated to New York City in 1890. Five years later, the *New York World* sponsored a competition to identify the ten best songwriters in the United States, and Davis was awarded second place. Approximately three hundred of his six hundred sacred, comic, and lyrical love songs were published. Several were extremely popular, including "In the Baggage Coach Ahead," which sold more than one million copies.

Figure C.21. Gussie Davis (1863–1899). On the cover of *Successful Songs by Gussie L. Davis*, 1899, Library of Congress, Music Division. Public domain.

Figure C.22. Edmond Dédé (c. 1827–1901). Louisiana Music Collection, Amistad Research Center, New Orleans, LA. Public domain.

Edmond Dédé (c. 1827–1901) was an American violinist, composer, and conductor born into a free Black family in New Orleans. As a young violin prodigy, he worked as a cigar roller to save enough money to relocate to Paris and study at the Conservatory. Upon arriving in France, he immediately began publishing his own works and conducting their premieres with L'Alcazar Orchestre. Dédé held this conducting position for more than twenty years and garnered significant international acclaim. In 1893, he returned to the United States to tour but left in 1894 due to systemic racial inequities and segregation. His song "La patriotisme" is a musical farewell mourning the shortcomings of his country of origin. His compositional output includes more than 250 songs, orchestral works, and an opera.

Figure C.23. Eugène Dédé (1867–1919). On the cover of *Chiffonnette: polka pour piano*, Op. 236, Bibliothèque nationale de France. Public domain.

Eugène Dédé (1867–1919) was a French composer who was the son of the renowned conductor and composer Edmond Dédé. His compositions include orchestral and piano works. There is currently no other known information about his life or career.

Figure C.24. Robert Nathaniel Dett (1882–1943). Library of Congress, Prints and Photographs Division, LC-DIG-ppmsca-17487. Public domain.

Robert Nathaniel Dett (1882–1943) was a Canadian American composer, teacher, pianist, organist, author, and conductor who was the first Black student to graduate from the Oberlin College Conservatory. He taught at several historically Black colleges and universities for decades and established the Hampton Institute's BS degree in music during his tenure as the chairman of the music department. Dett's profound pedagogical legacy also included his choir, which he transformed from an amateur community group into an internationally renowned touring ensemble. Dett was the recipient of numerous awards for his compositions and literary writings, and he frequently advocated for the importance of preserving Black American folk music traditions. He wrote, "It is doubtful if anywhere in the world a race of people ever were so publicly derided in story, drama, and song as the Negro in America." Dett's compositions include more than one hundred works for piano, organ, chorus, solo voice, orchestra, and an oratorio.

Figure C.25. Sophia Dussek (b. 1775). "Sophia Corri" by unknown artist, EU0512. © University of Edinburgh Art Collection.

Sophia Dussek (b. 1775) was an English harpist, singer, and composer who made her debut singing at the Salomon concerts under the direction of Franz Joseph Haydn in 1791. She later premiered Haydn's *The Storm* and was a soloist in the London premiere of Wolfgang Amadeus Mozart's *Requiem* at Covent Garden. After moving to Paddington in 1812, she founded a music school and published extensively. Her compositional output is primarily for harp and consists of several collections of sonatas as well as themes and variations on popular tunes. Additionally, she wrote sonatas for keyboard and violin, a piano sonata, and a sonata for keyboard, violin, and German flute. Until recently, her C Minor Harp Sonata was erroneously attributed to her husband Jan Ladislav Dussek.

Figure C.26. Mademoiselle Duval (1718–after 1775). Cover of Duval's *Les Génies ou Les caractères de L'Amour*. Public domain.

Mademoiselle Duval (1718–after 1775) was a French composer, dancer, singer, and harpsichordist. Her 1736 ballet-héroïque *Les Génies, ou Les caractères de l'Amour* was the second opera by a woman to be performed at the Paris Opera. *Les Génies* ran for a series of nine performances, and the November 1736 *Mercure de France* reported that the piece was "varied and extremely well developed in many respects." Duval was also respected as a harpsichordist, and she played for all nine performances of her opera. The same issue of the *Mercure de France* recounted that "to the astonishment and pleasure of the Public, this young person seated in the orchestra, accompanied her entire Opera from the Overture to the last Note." Reports of her other musical activities are less conclusive, as Duval was a very common French surname.

Figure C.27. Justin Elie (1883–1931). On the cover of *Les Chants de la Montagne*, No. 2: Nostalgie, 1922. Public domain.

Justin Elie (1883–1931) was one of the most renowned Haitian composers in the early twentieth century. After studies at the Paris Conservatory, he returned to Haiti to pursue a musical career, presenting recitals in Cuba, Jamaica, St. Thomas, Curaçao, Venezuela, Puerto Rico, and the Dominican Republic. Earning a living as a musician in Latin America was difficult at the time, so Elie ultimately moved to New York City to pursue more financially lucrative opportunities. He often conducted his own orchestral works on *The Lure of the Tropics*, the weekly radio program he hosted. Additionally, Elie wrote music for numerous silent films and musical dramas. Many of his orchestral and theatrical works were inspired by Latin American folklore, the vodou religious ceremony, and traditions of the African diaspora.

Figure C.28. Louise Farrenc (1804–1875). Bibliothèque nationale de France. Public domain.

Louise Farrenc (1804–1875) was a French composer, pianist, educator, and scholar who was the second woman to hold a permanent piano professorship at the Paris Conservatory. Many of her students had successful musical careers, and the Conservatory adopted her collection of etudes in all the major and minor keys as part of the required curriculum for pianists. In addition to solo piano works, Farrenc also composed orchestral overtures, symphonies, and chamber music. She was awarded the Chartier Prize for her chamber music in 1861 and 1869, and she collaborated with her husband, Aristide, to compile and edit *Le trésor des pianistes*. Farrenc was an advocate for reviving keyboard music from the seventeenth and eighteenth centuries, and she hosted *séances historiques* in which she and her students performed historical works. Her research gave her tremendous insight into the nuances and challenges of historical performance practice, and she published a manual on baroque ornamentation.

Figure C.29. Chiquinha Gonzaga (1847–1935). Coleção Edinha Diniz/Acervo Instituto Moreira Salles. Public domain.

Chiquinha Gonzaga (1847–1935) was a Brazilian composer, a pianist, and the first woman to conduct an orchestra in Brazil. In addition to publishing more than three hundred songs and dances, Gonzaga also collaborated with the most renowned Brazilian playwrights of the time to compose seventy-seven stage works dealing primarily with topics of daily life. Many of her works were exceedingly popular during her lifetime, such as her 1912 stage work *Forrobodó*, which was performed fifteen hundred times. Gonzaga also assisted with founding the Brazilian Society of Theater Authors, enthusiastically advocated for the end of slavery in Brazil, and was a leading figure in the Brazilian suffragist movement. Gonzaga was a single mother for much of her career, and her personal life was frequently chastised. Despite societal expectations, she proudly supported her children by performing, composing, and teaching.

Figure C.30. Anna Gardner Goodwin (1874–1959). Irvine Garland Penn and John Wesley Edward Bowen, eds., *The United Negro: His Problems and His Progress* (D. E. Luther Publishing Co., 1902). Public domain.

Anna Gardner Goodwin (1874–1959) was an American educator, pianist, and composer of sacred music and marches. An advocate for the education of other Black musicians, she taught music with her husband at Morehouse College, where she also accompanied the school's glee club. Her final composition, "Freedom to All March," was written after approximately four thousand White protestors attacked an apartment building housing a Black family during the 1951 Riot of Cicero.

Figure C.31. Maud Cuney Hare (1874–1936). Maud Cuney Hare, *Norris Wright Cuney: A Tribune of the Black People* (Crisis Publishing Co., 1913). Public domain.

Maud Cuney Hare (1874–1936) was an American musicologist, pianist, teacher, and playwright who dedicated much of her career to studying the works of other Black musicians. Her 1936 *Negro Musicians and Their Music* was the first major twentieth-century survey of Black music, and Hare was the foremost authority on Black American music during her lifetime. Hare's research included extensive travel throughout Louisiana, Mexico, and the Caribbean to collect folk songs. She later arranged these songs for voice and piano in publications that included her own translations of the texts and detailed critical commentary. Hare also toured frequently as a pianist, published scholarly articles, was the music critic of *The Crisis*, and was a political activist.

Figure C.32. Henry Hart (1839–1915). Cover of Hart's *On the Beautiful Lake Erie*, Library of Congress, American Sheet Music Collection. Public domain.

Henry Hart (1839–1915) was an American composer, singer, and violinist born into a free Black family. He moved to Indianapolis, Indiana, around the turn of the twentieth century and quickly advanced through the musical and social ranks of the city. In 1901, the *Indianapolis News* described Hart as a "social necessity," and he and his wife Sarah taught their children music and formed a family performing ensemble that became quite popular. His published compositions include works for piano, solo voice, and chorus.

Figure C.33. Fanny Mendelssohn Hensel (1805–1847); Moritz Daniel Oppenheim, 1842. Courtesy of the Leo Baeck Institute. Public domain.

Fanny Mendelssohn Hensel (1805–1847) was a German pianist and prolific composer of more than 450 stage, orchestral, chamber, keyboard, choral, and vocal works. Although her family endeavored to curtail her public professional career, she continued to hone her craft for the duration of her life. Throughout the nineteenth and twentieth centuries, several of Hensel's works were misattributed to her brother Felix. For example, a few of Hensel's lieder were published under Felix's name in the 1820s, purportedly as a way for her works to be distributed without drawing socially inappropriate public attention to a woman of her social standing. As a pianist, Hensel was praised for her prodigious memory, and she dazzled audiences at private salon performances in her home.

Figure C.34. Élisabeth Jacquet de La Guerre (1665–1729); François de Troy, c. 1700. Heritage Image Partnership, Alamy Stock Photo.

Élisabeth Jacquet de La Guerre (1665–1729) was a French harpsichordist, composer, and teacher who was the first woman to have a work staged at the Paris Opera. Born into a family of prominent Parisian harpsichord builders and musicians, she was presented to Louis XIV as a young child. The King was captivated by her musical abilities and arranged for her continued education. He also supported her composition career for the rest of his life, even after Jacquet de La Guerre left the court to be married. Throughout her career, Jacquet de La Guerre was respected as a virtuosic performer. A 1677 account in the *Mercure galant* reported that "she sings at sight the most difficult music. She accompanies herself, and accompanies others who wish to sing, at the harpsichord, which she plays in a manner that cannot be imitated." Jacquet de La Guerre published harpsichord works, violin sonatas, an opera, a ballet, and instrumental chamber music. She also hosted regular salon performances to showcase new works by the leading composers of the day.

Figure C.35. Francis Johnson (1792–1844); Robert Douglass Jr., nineteenth century. Wikimedia, public domain.

Francis Johnson (1792–1844) was an American violinist, Kent-bugle player, bandmaster, and composer of more than two hundred works. He was the first Black American to publish sheet music, one of the first Americans to perform in racially integrated concerts, and one of the earliest composers of cotillions. Born to a free Black family in Pennsylvania, Johnson became the band leader for the Philadelphia State Fencibles in 1821. He and his band performed at prestigious events throughout the 1820s, including the annual birthday celebrations of George Washington. Johnson then traveled to London and Paris with his band, where he played for Queen Victoria and was gifted a silver bugle. Johnson brought the English concept of the promenade concert back to the United States, and massive crowds enjoyed this style of concert on his subsequent United States tours. His funeral was reportedly one of the largest witnessed in Philadelphia at the time.

Figure C.36. Sydney Lambert (1838–1905). Cover of Lambert's *Transports Joyeux*, Op. 16. Public domain.

Sydney Lambert (1838–1905) was an American composer and pianist born into an established musical family of free Creoles in New Orleans. He began his musical career playing the piano in the pit of the Théâtre d'Orléans, before relocating to Europe to work as a court musician in Portugal. In the 1870s, the King of Portugal honored Lambert for writing a piano method. Lambert later taught in Paris and published at least thirty-two works.

Figure C.37. Josephine Lang (1815–1880); Carl Müller, c. 1842. Heinrich Adolf Köstlin, Josefine Lang: Lebensabriss, 1881. Public domain.

Josephine Lang (1815–1880) was a German pianist, singer, teacher, and composer of approximately 150 art songs. Born into a family of professional musicians, Lang made her piano debut at age eleven and began composing around 1828. Somewhat isolated by her parents and in poor health, Lang developed her considerable musical abilities primarily through self-study and occasional private tutors. Lang began teaching piano lessons while still a child in order to supplement her family's income, and she frequently performed at parties. Felix Mendelssohn gave her lessons in counterpoint and harmony and inspired her to pursue a professional career beyond salon performances. Both he and his sister Fanny Hensel remained champions of Lang's works for years to come, with Felix using several of Lang's songs as inspiration for his own improvisations. Robert Schumann also publicly praised Lang's songs, many of which were published during her lifetime.

Figure C.38. Ida M. Larkins (fl. 1905). First page of Larkin's *Wild Flowers*. Public domain.

Ida M. Larkins (fl. 1905) was an American composer of solo piano music and songs at the turn of the twentieth century. She collaborated with her husband John Larkins to write popular songs for vaudeville teams, including Bert Williams and George Walker. Additionally, she wrote and published a waltz, which is one of the earliest known solo piano works by a Black American woman.

Figure C.39. Luise Adolpha Le Beau (1850–1927) in 1872. Luise Adolpha Le Beau, Lebenserinnerungen einer Komponistin, 1910. Public domain.

Luise Adolpha Le Beau (1850–1927) was a German composer, pianist, and music critic whose compositional output includes two operas, an oratorio, lieder, a piano concerto, instrumental chamber music, solo piano pieces, and choral works. She made her piano debut as a teenager with the Baden court orchestra, won numerous prizes for her compositions and performances, and received consistently favorable reviews. Later in her career, Le Beau wrote critical reviews for *Allgemeine deutsche Musik-Zeitung* and the Baden-Baden newspaper. She also founded a private music class aimed at training young women to become piano instructors. Le Beau's memoirs were published as *Lebenserinnerungen einer Komponistin* in 1910.

Figure C.40. Franziska Lebrun (1756–1791); Thomas Gainsborough, 1780. Bridgeman images. Art Gallery of South Australia.

Franziska Lebrun (1756–1791) was a German soprano and composer who worked as a chamber musician in the Munich court, held the title *virtuosa da camera* for her operatic singing in Mannheim, and concertized extensively throughout Europe. She made appearances at La Scala in Milan, the Concert Spirituel in Paris, the King's Theatre in London, the Viennese Burgtheater, the Neapolitan Teatro S Carlo, and the carnivals in Berlin. During her time in London, she composed and published two sets of sonatas for violin and keyboard. These works were distributed in Paris, Amsterdam, Offenbach, Berlin, Mannheim, and Worms.

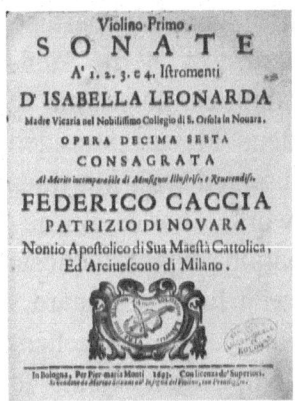

Figure C.41. Isabella Leonarda (1620–1704). Cover of Leonarda's *Sonate a' 1, 2, 3, e 4 istromenti*. Public domain.

Isabella Leonarda (1620–1704) was an Italian composer who lived and worked in the Ursuline convent Collegio di S. Orsola in Novara from 1636 until her death. She held numerous positions at the convent, including music instructor, mother and clerk, mother superior, *madre vicaria*, and counsellor. Leonarda composed approximately two hundred works in nearly every sacred genre of her time, ranging from small instrumental sonatas to large, concerted masses and psalm settings. It is possible that she wrote some of the texts for her sacred non-liturgical works, and her 1693 collection of instrumental pieces is the earliest known published book of sonatas by a woman. A sonnet by A. Saminiati Lucchese laudably compared Leonarda's musical abilities to the military prowess of Emperor Leopold I.

Figure C.42. Liliuokalani (1838–1917). Library of Congress, Prints and Photographs Division, LC-USZ62-22488. Public domain.

Liliuokalani (1838–1917) was the only queen regnant and the last sovereign monarch of the Hawaiian Kingdom, over which she reigned from 1891 to 1893. She played a variety of plucked instruments and was a composer, pianist, organist, and choir director. In her autobiography, Liliuokalani writes that "to compose was as natural to me as to breathe," and she credits herself with being the first Hawaiian to successfully compose using Western musical notation. Most of Liliuokalani's compositions are songs, and she endeavored to blend musical elements of Hawaiian and Western European traditions.

Figure C.43. María Malibrán (1808–1836); from the portrait by Leon Viardot, c. 1825. Henry Edward Krehbiel, "The Original Zerlina in New York," in *A Book of Operas: Their Histories, Their Plots and Their Music*, 1909. Public domain.

María Malibrán (1808–1836) was a Spanish composer and singer who rose to extraordinary stardom during her career on opera stages in London, Paris, Rome, Naples, New York, and Milan. In spite of her father's notoriously abusive teaching methods, Malibrán developed an impeccable technique and noteworthy vocal range that allowed her to sing contralto and soprano roles. Revered in leading roles on the stage until her tragic death in a riding accident, Malibrán was described in the *Manchester Guardian* in 1836 as "the prima donna whom thousands have worshipped," who was "looked upon as the goddess of song during her brief existence." In addition to performing, Malibrán composed numerous romances for voice and piano. Her contemporaries called her "La Sévigné de la romance," and her songs were praised by Hector Berlioz and Robert Schumann.

Figure C.44. Marianna Martines (1744–1812); Anton von Maron, c. 1773. Wien Museum.

Marianna Martines (1744–1812) was an Austrian singer, keyboardist, and composer whose father's position as *maestro di camera* at the Viennese papal embassy gave her access to the most prominent musicians of her time. Franz Joseph Haydn and Wolfgang Amadeus Mozart attended the salons she hosted in her home, and Mozart collaborated with Martines at least once in performing a four-hand keyboard work. Charles Burney heard her sing in 1772 and wrote that her tone, intonation, expressiveness, and ornamentation were "more perfect than any singer I had ever heard." He also praised her as a composer, referring to her as "a most excellent contrapuntist" and taking copies of several of her compositions home to London. Nearly seventy of her rumored two hundred musical works are extant, including masses, litanies, psalms, oratorios, motets, arias, cantatas, concertos, overtures, and sonatas.

Figure C.45. Emilie Mayer (1812–1883); Eduard Meyer, after a drawing by Pauline Suhrlandt, nineteenth century. Wikimedia, public domain.

Emilie Mayer (1812–1883) was a German composer and sculptor who wrote stage works, symphonies, overtures, instrumental chamber music, piano sonatas, choral works, and art songs. She was highly respected as a composer during her lifetime, and her music was performed in Brussels, Lyons, Budapest, Dessau, Halle, Leipzig, and Munich. Additionally, several of her songs were published in voice books intended for at-home performances. Although it was rare for a woman to have public performances of orchestral works, Mayer's symphonies were consistently praised. Carl Loewe wrote that her B Minor Symphony was "an important and ingenious work of art with which the talented artist has enriched musical literature." A review of a later performance of the same piece in the *Neue Berliner Musikzeitung* declared that Mayer "is a female composer who not only writes for the piano, but also solves the difficult task of orchestral composition . . . the composer knows how to organize the instruments, to measure their force against each other and to mix their tone colors effectively."

Figure C.46. Anacleto de Medeiros (1866–1907). Musica Brasilis. Public domain.

Anacleto de Medeiros (1866–1907) was a Brazilian composer, conductor, and multi-instrumentalist. After studying the piccolo as a child, he pursued an education at the Brazilian Conservatory, where he specialized in the soprano saxophone and mastered most wind instruments. In 1896, he formed the Banda do Corpo de Bombeiros, with whom he produced some of the first professional recordings in Brazil. In 1904, the ensemble recorded Medeiros's waltz *Farrula* for Odeon Records. Further recordings of his works in 1906 and 1908 were released on Victor Records. His compositions include polkas, *xotes*, and waltzes.

Figure C.47. Françoise-Charlotte de Senneterre Ménétou (1679–1745). Bibliothèque nationale de France. Public domain.

Françoise-Charlotte de Senneterre Ménétou (1679–1745) was a French singer, dancer, harpsichordist, and composer who was the youngest woman to have an entire collection of her works published in France. Potentially a student of François Couperin, Ménétou likely inspired Couperin's "La Ménétou," the first movement of his 1717 *Septième Ordre*. Ménétou had close family connections to the court, and at age nine she was presented to Louis XIV and the Dauphine Marie Anne. Her performance provided great amusement to the King, and he found her playing to be "délicieuse." Six of Ménétou's airs can be found in a 1689 manuscript alongside works by Jean-Henri d'Anglebert, Michel Lambert, Nicolas Lebègue, and Jean-Baptiste Lully. In 1691, Ménétou published *Recueil d'airs*, a book of fifteen airs printed by Christophe Ballard.

Figure C.48. Presumed portrait of Hélène de Montgeroult (1764–1836); attrib. Louis-Philippe Joseph Girod de Vienney, c. 1800–1825. © Musée des Beaux-Arts de Tours, photo by D. Couineau.

Hélène de Montgeroult (1764–1836) was a virtuosic French pianist, educator, *salonnière*, and composer who endeavored to imitate the Italian bel canto style on the piano. A revered pedagogue, she was appointed professor of piano at the newly established Paris Conservatory in 1795. It would be a half century before another woman, Louise Farrenc, would be appointed to such a substantial piano teaching position at the Conservatory. Montgeroult also taught in her Parisian home and hosted numerous salons where the most prominent musicians of her time gathered. Her compositional output includes piano sonatas, vocal works, and an extensive three-volume piano method. The first volume is composed of 927 exercises, and the remaining two volumes contain 114 etudes, variations, a canon, fugues, and a fantasy.

Figure C.49. Anna Caroline Oury (1808–1880); Camille Silvy, 1861. © National Portrait Gallery, London.

Anna Caroline Oury (1808–1880) was a German pianist and composer who wrote more than 180 dances and fantasies for piano. After studies in Munich, Vienna, and Augsburg, she began an extensive touring career that took her to France, Poland, Germany, Austria, England, Russia, the Netherlands, Italy, and Belgium. Oury heard Ludwig van Beethoven improvise in her teens and later made her London debut with Nicolò Paganini. Before settling in England and devoting herself to composition, she toured for eight years with her husband, the violinist Antonio James Oury.

Figure C.50. Maria Theresia von Paradis (1759–1824); Faustine Parmantié, 1784. Österreichische Nationalbibliothek Bildarchiv und Grafiksammlung.

Maria Theresia von Paradis (1759–1824) was an Austrian singer, composer, pianist, organist, and teacher. Her extant compositions include art songs, operas, and cantatas; her solo piano works and concertos are lost. Paradis was a respected performer in Viennese salons and concert halls, and Wolfgang Amadeus Mozart and Antonio Salieri may have composed keyboard concertos for her. On one of Paradis's tours, the *Journal de Paris* reviewed her, saying, "One must have heard her to form an idea of the touch, the precision, the fluency and vividness of her playing." As a young child Paradis became blind, and during her extended visits to Paris for tours, she assisted with forming the first school for the blind. In 1808, Paradis also opened a music school for girls in Vienna, where she taught her students piano, singing, and music theory.

Figure C.51. Maria Hester Park (1760–1813). Cover of Park's Sonata, Op. 7. Public domain.

Maria Hester Park (1760–1813) was an English composer, teacher, and keyboardist who gave numerous public concerts and taught music to noble families. Park's students included the Duchess of Devonshire and her two daughters. At age twenty-two, Park made her debut performing a harpsichord concerto in the Hanover Square concert series in London. She continued to perform throughout the 1780s in London and the surrounding areas and corresponded with and exchanged copies of sonatas with Franz Joseph Haydn. Of the thirteen collections of keyboard and vocal works Park composed, three were published by subscription. More than three hundred people subscribed to her first book of accompanied keyboard sonatas, including the music historian Charles Burney.

Figure C.52. Maria Frances Parke (1772–1822). Cover of Parke's Sonatas, Op. 1. Public domain.

Maria Frances Parke (1772–1822) was an English singer, pianist, and composer who was a leading soprano soloist in concerts and oratorios throughout England. She made her harpsichord debut at the age of eight and her piano and singing debut the following year, playing a piano concerto by Johann Samuel Schroeter for her father's benefit concert. Although critics praised her keyboard abilities and predicted she would become "one of the best Piano Forte performers in England," she ultimately pursued a career as a singer. Parke sang in the Handel Commemoration concerts in 1784 and for Franz Joseph Haydn's benefit concert in 1794. Her compositions include five piano sonatas, a divertimento and rondo, and three vocal works.

Figure C.53. Julie Pinel (fl. 1710–1737). Cover of Pinel's *Nouveau recueil d'airs sérieux et à boire*. Public domain.

Julie Pinel (fl. 1710–1737) was a French composer who was likely a member of the Pinel family of court lutenists in the service of the house of Soubise. In 1736, she acquired an eight-year royal privilege to publish her vocal and instrumental chamber music. Her only extant work is a 1737 book of airs for voice, flute, and continuo. In the dedication to that book, Pinel wrote that she would next compose a book of cantatas. Several primary sources also suggest that Pinel may have composed *Apollonius,* a five-act opera that is lost and was neither published nor performed.

Figure C.54. Loïsa Puget (1810–1889); Marie-Alexandre Alophe, c. 1850–1970. Bibliothèque nationale de France. Public domain.

Loïsa Puget (1810–1889) was a French composer and singer who wrote three hundred romances and was regarded by Henri-Louis Blanchard as the "queen of this genre." Annual illustrated volumes of her songs were published each year between 1833 and 1853, and translations of her works appeared in England, Germany, and the United States. Her most famous romance was "À la grâce de Dieu," which inspired dramatic works by Gaetano Donizetti and Adolphe d'Ennery. Composers including Karl Czerny, Henri Rosellen, and Franz Hünten published virtuosic keyboard adaptations of her songs, further increasing her renown. Additionally, Puget's songs were frequently performed in convents, girls' boarding schools, and salons. She also composed two one-act operas, solo piano works, and a set of quadrilles for four hands.

Figure C.55. Louise Reichardt (1779–1826). Cover of Reichardt's *Zwoelf Gesänge*, Op. 3. Public domain.

Louise Reichardt (1779–1826) was a German composer and singing teacher whose nearly seventy-five songs were published during her lifetime. Several of her songs were so popular that they continued to be printed in anthologies for fifty years after her death. Reichardt was mostly self-taught, reading literary works and studying scores by the numerous intellectuals and musicians her father entertained in their home. Her colleagues praised her beautiful melodies, and her songs were admired by the poets whose texts she set. A respected pedagogue, Reichardt maintained a private voice studio and conducted women's choruses. She was responsible for preparing the singers for Hamburg's music festival, where George Frideric Handel's *Messiah* and Wolfgang Amadeus Mozart's *Requiem* were performed for six thousand people. Reichardt also founded a singing club dedicated to performing Handel's oratorios. In this capacity, she coached the soloists, directed the rehearsals, and made German translations of the English texts.

Figure C.56. Henriette Renié (1875–1956). From Jaymee Haefner, ed., *The Legend of Henriette Renié* (Authorhouse, 2006), 42. © 2006 Jaymee Haefner. Reprinted with permission.

Henriette Renié (1875–1956) was a French harpist, pedagogue, and composer whose harp concerto helped to establish the harp as a solo instrument in an orchestral context. Renié won a first prize at the Paris Conservatory at age eleven, and she was subsequently the first young woman allowed to participate in the Conservatory's composition and fugue classes. She began working professionally while still a student, attending classes in the morning, teaching lessons in the afternoon, and playing at parties most evenings. Throughout her career, she toured with the Orchestre Lamoureux and collaborated with many important musicians, including Pablo Casals, Gabrielle Pierne, and Maurice Ravel. Renié maintained a large private studio and wrote a *Méthode complete de harpe*, which is still used today. She was also appointed a Knight in the Légion d'Honneur and created the first international harp competition in 1914.

Figure C.57. Clara Kathleen Rogers (1844–1931). Clara Kathleen Rogers, *Memories of a Musical Career*, 1919. Public domain.

Clara Kathleen Rogers (1844–1931) was an English American singer, composer, and teacher who published six books on vocal technique and lyric diction. Although she was forbidden from formally studying composition at the Leipzig Conservatory due to her gender, she graduated with honors after studying piano, violin, cello, part-writing, and harmony. Rogers was born into a family of prominent musicians, and she made her singing debut in Turin before touring Italy, England, and the United States. After her marriage, she permanently relocated to the United States to focus on composing, writing, and teaching at the New England Conservatory. Her compositional output includes art songs and instrumental chamber music. Reviews for Rogers's music and pedagogical manuals were quite favorable. The *New York Times* urged every singing teacher and student to read her 1893 *The Philosophy of Singing* "for its high and valuable thought upon the purpose of vocal art." Likewise, the year before her death, an article in *Art Song in America* asserted that "there is a spontaneity about her songs whose equal is far to seek in the songs of her day."

Figure C.58. Ignatius Sancho (c. 1729–1780); Francesco Bartolozzi, after Thomas Gainsborough, 1781. © National Maritime Museum, Greenwich, London.

Ignatius Sancho (c. 1729–1780) was an English composer born to an enslaved woman on a ship en route from Guinea to Cartagena, Colombia. After being relocated to England, Sancho worked as a servant for several noble families. During this time, he learned to read and write and was introduced to prominent literary, artistic, and musical circles. By 1773, he had earned enough money to leave domestic service and open a grocery store and oil supply business in Westminster. His shop became a popular meeting place for some of the most influential artists, writers, actors, and politicians of his time. Known during his life as "the extraordinary Negro," Sancho was a prominent abolitionist, and his published letters addressing enslavement sold widely. Additionally, he owned property, which allowed him to become the first known person of African origin to vote in British parliamentary elections. His compositional output includes a collection of songs and three sets of instrumental country dances. A *Theory of Music* is also attributed to him, although it is no longer extant.

Jane Savage (c. 1752–1824) was an English composer, singer, and keyboardist who studied music alongside her father's students and became a skilled composer of vocal and keyboard music. Savage's 1785 setting of the "Hymn for Christmas Day" is the earliest known Anglican hymn setting by a woman; it was recently discovered in a collection of music written to be performed by women and girls in charity hospitals. Savage also worked as the organist for the Asylum, an orphanage for girls in London. Savage assumed financial responsibility for the publication of her works, most of which were written before 1793.

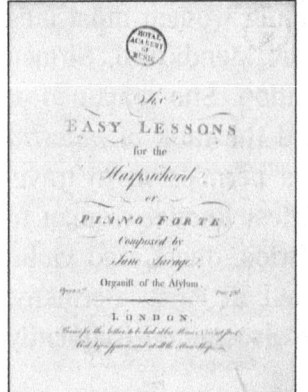

Figure C.59. Jane Savage (c. 1752–1824). Cover of Savage's *Six Easy Lessons*, Op. 2. Public domain.

Figure C.60. Corona Schröter (1751–1802); Anton Graff, 1787. Klassik Stiftung Weimar, Museen, Inv.-Nr.:G41, photo: Klaus G. Beyer.

Corona Schröter (1751–1802) was a German singer, actress, and composer who captivated Leipzig audiences beginning in 1765 with her appearances in Johann Adam Hiller's Grand Concerts. Her admirers noted her purity of vocal tone and her emotional delivery. As a chamber musician for Duchess Anna Amalia of Saxe-Weimar, she performed in many of Johann Wolfgang von Goethe's dramas. She also composed the music and premiered the title role in Goethe's 1782 Singspiel *Die Fischerin*. Schröter published two collections of songs, the first of which she announced in Carl Friedrich Cramer's *Magazin der Musik*. Schröter wrote: "I have had to overcome much hesitation before I seriously decided to publish a collection of short poems that I have provided with melodies. A certain feeling towards propriety and morality is stamped upon our sex, which does not allow us to appear alone in public, and without an escort: Thus, how can I present this, my musical work to the public, other than with timidity?"

Figure C.61. Clara Wieck Schumann (1819–1896); Andreas Staub, c. 1839. Berthed Litzmann, Clara Schumann, 1913. Public domain.

Clara Wieck Schumann (1819–1896) was a German pianist, teacher, and composer of two piano concertos, chamber music, solo piano works, and art songs. Born into a family of musicians, she studied with the most respected teachers in Leipzig, Dresden, and Berlin. She also attended every major performance in Leipzig and learned how to manage the business aspects of a musical career. A piano prodigy, Schumann debuted at the Leipzig Gewandhaus at age nine, performed in Paris at age twelve, and appeared in Vienna at age eighteen. She continued to gain international acclaim as a concert pianist, giving extensive tours throughout Western Europe and Russia. After her husband Robert's death, Schumann continued to tour, edited the authoritative publication of her husband's collected compositions, and was appointed principal piano teacher at the Hoch Conservatory in Frankfurt.

Figure C.62. Maddalena Laura Sirmen (1745–1818). © Comune di Milano, tutti i diritti riservati-Raccolta delle Stampe "Achille Bertarelli," Castello Sforzesco, Milano.

Maddalena Laura Sirmen (1745–1818) was an Italian composer, violinist, and singer who did not have the privilege of being born into either a family of musicians or the aristocracy. Of her own determination coupled with good fortune, she became an internationally acclaimed musician and achieved significant financial success. Due to a shortage of young women musicians residing in the Venetian Ospedale di San Lazzaro dei Mendicanti, Sirmen entered the institution at age seven by musical audition. She remained at the Mendicanti for fourteen years, where she reached the rank of *maestra* and became a skilled enough violinist to be granted permission to travel for lessons with Giuseppe Tartini. Sirmen is the earliest known woman to write string quartets, and she also composed string trios, duets, and violin concertos. Copies of her music were widely circulated in Paris, Germany, London, Naples, Finland, and the United States. She also toured frequently across Western Europe and Russia.

Figure C.63. Barbara Strozzi (1619–1677); Bernardo Strozzi, c. 1640. Erich Lessing/Art Resource, NY. Staatliche Kunstsammlungen, Dresden

Barbara Strozzi (1619–1677) was a Venetian composer and singer who published eight collections of music and is often credited with creating the cantata genre. The adopted daughter of the famed poet Giulio Strozzi, she grew up in a household surrounded by the most prominent intellectuals and musicians of her day. Barbara began her performance career in 1634, singing informally for members of the elite Accademia degli Incogniti, an intellectual organization of musicians, writers, and philosophers known for promoting opera. Several years later, her father founded the Accademia degli Unisoni to promote performances of Barbara's works. Participating in Academy meetings was taboo for a woman, and like many women performers, Barbara's chastity was debated in vitriolic satires. Strozzi published 125 pieces for voice and continuo without the financial support of a court position, church appointment, or wealthy patron.

Figure C.64. Germaine Tailleferre (1892–1983). © Bru Zane Mediabase. Used by permission.

Germaine Tailleferre (1892–1983) was a French composer, teacher, and pianist who studied at the Paris Conservatory against the wishes of her father and was the only woman in Les Six, a group of prominent composers who wrote in a distinctive neoclassical style. Her early compositions were promoted by Erik Satie and the Princesse Edmond de Polignac, the latter of whom commissioned Tailleferre's piano concerto. After the 1920s, difficulties in Tailleferre's personal life forced her to compose rapidly and primarily by commission. Although she was insecure about her creative abilities during these years, she wrote a significant amount of successful film music, and her mid-century operas were quite well-received. Tailleferre taught for most of her life and was particularly devoted to music for children. Her compositional output includes operas, ballets, incidental music, film and television scores, orchestral and wind band works, choral pieces and songs, instrumental chamber music, and solo piano works.

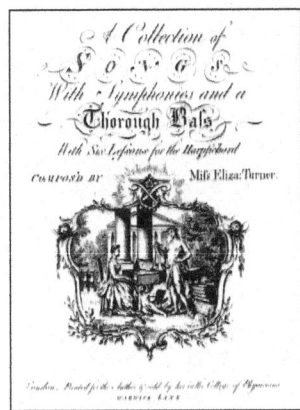

Figure C.65. Elizabeth Turner (d. 1756). Cover of Turner's *A Collection of Songs with Symphonies and a Thorough Bass with Six Lessons for the Harpsichord*. Public domain.

Elizabeth Turner (d. 1756) was a composer and singer who was one of the earliest known Englishwomen to publish a substantial collection of musical works. More than four hundred people subscribed to her 1750 volume of songs, and her 1756 collection of songs and harpsichord lessons had at least 350 subscribers. The subscription lists included elite patrons as well as prominent musicians such as George Frideric Handel, William Boyce, and John Stanley. Several of her songs were popular enough to appear in *London Magazine* and *The Lady's Magazine,* the latter of which dubbed her "the ingenious Miss Eliza Turner." Her songs continued to appear in print as late as 1795, decades after her death. Turner was more well-known during her lifetime as a soprano than a composer, and critics praised her aria performances in works by Handel, Boyce, and Thomas Arne. Upon her death, the *London Evening Post* wrote that her "extraordinary Genius and Abilities in Musick, make her justly lamented by all Lovers of Harmony."

Figure C.66. Virginie Morel-du Verger (1799–1870). Cover of Morel-du Verger's *Huit etudes mélodiques*.

Virginie Morel-du Verger (1799–1870) was a French pianist and composer. She entered the Paris Conservatory in 1814 to study with Louis Adam and was awarded a first prize in piano. She later studied with Ferdinand Hummel and was a pianist for the Duchess de Berry. Her compositional output includes a piano sonata and etudes, violin and piano duets, and other chamber works.

Figure C.67. José White (1836–1918). James Monroe Trotter, *Music and Some Highly Musical People*, 1878. Public domain.

José White (1836–1918) was a Cuban violin virtuoso and composer who spent much of his career in Paris. After competing against sixty other candidates, he was unanimously accepted by the faculty to study violin at the Paris Conservatory in 1855. He won a first prize the next year, and the review of his performance in *Le Pays* reported that White "performed with an extraordinary animation, not like a pupil but as a great artist who commands his audience." In the ensuing decades, he toured extensively in Cuba, South America, the United States, and Western Europe. He eventually earned the position of court violinist to the emperor Dom Pedro II of Brazil, where he cofounded the Sociedade de Conciertos Clásicos. His works include a violin concerto, a string quartet, a bolero for violin and orchestra, variations for harpsichord and orchestra, violin etudes, and several pieces for violin and piano.

BIBLIOGRAPHY

Adams, Andrew. "Voicing the Silent Language of the Soul: The Life and Works of Clara Kathleen Rogers (1844–1931)." *Journal of Singing* 67, no. 3 (Jan/Feb 2011): 257–66.

Andrews, Joyce. "Amanda Aldridge, Teacher and Composer: A Life in Music." *Journal of Singing* 66, no. 3 (Jan/Feb 2010): 253–68.

Angermüller, Rudolph, Hidemi Matsushita, and Ron Rabin. "Paradis [Paradies], Maria Theresia." In *Grove Music Online*. Oxford University Press, 2001. https://doi.org/10.1093/gmo/9781561592630.article.20868.

Anthony, James R. "Duval, Mlle." In *The Norton/Grove Dictionary of Women Composers*, edited by Julie Anne Sadie and Rhian Samuel. New York: W. W. Norton, 1994.

Arnold, Elsie, and Jane Baldauf-Berdes. *Maddalena Lombardini Sirmen: Eighteenth-Century Composer, Violinist, and Businesswoman*. London: Scarecrow, 2002.

Baldassarre, Antonio. "Music, Painting, and Domestic Life: Hortense de Beauharnais in Arenenberg." *Music in Art* 23, no. 1/2 (Spring–Fall 1998): 49–61.

Baldwin, Olive, and Thelma Wilson. "Abrams, Harriett." In *Grove Music Online*. Oxford University Press, 2001. https://doi.org/10.1093/gmo/9781561592630.article.00059.

———. "Parke family." In *Grove Music Online*. Oxford University Press, 2001. https://doi.org/10.1093/gmo/9781561592630.article.20919.

Banat, Gabriel. *The Chevalier de Saint-Georges: Virtuoso of the Sword and the Bow*. Hillsdale, NY: Pendragon, 2006.

Banfield, Stephen, Jeremy Dibble, and Anya Laurence. "Coleridge-Taylor, Samuel." In *Grove Music Online*. Oxford University Press, 2013. https://doi.org/10.1093/gmo/9781561592630.article.A2248993.

Beer, Anna. *Sounds and Sweet Airs: The Forgotten Women of Classical Music*. London: Oneworld Publications, 2016.

Block, Adrienne Fried. *Amy Beach: Passionate Victorian*. New York: Oxford University Press, 1998.

Brain, Corisha. "A Social, Literary, and Musical Study of Julie Pinel's *Nouveau recueil d'airs sérieux et à boire* (Paris, 1737)." MM thesis, New Zealand School of Music, 2008.

Bridges, Thomas W. "Casulana [Mezari], Maddalena." In *Grove Music Online*. Oxford University Press, 2001. https://doi.org./10.1093/gmo/9781561592630.article.05155.

Brooks, Christopher. "Dett, R(obert) Nathaniel." In *Grove Music Online*. Oxford University Press, 2001. https://doi.org/10.1093/gmo/9781561592630.article.07669.

Burney, Charles. *An Account of the Musical Performances in Westminster-Abbey, and the Pantheon, May 26th, 27th, 29th, and June the 3rd and 5th, 1784: In Commemoration of Handel*. London, 1785.

Carter, Stewart Arlen. "The Music of Isabella Leonarda (1620–1704)." PhD diss., Stanford University, 1982.

Chung, David. "The Menetou Manuscript: A Study of Styles and Repertory for the Harpsichord During Late-Seventeenth-Century France." *Revue de Musicologie* 101, no. 2 (2015): 407–36.

Citron, Marcia J. "Chaminade, Cécile." In *Grove Music Online*. Oxford University Press, 2001. https://doi.org/10.1093/gmo/9781561592630.article.05388.

———. "Women and the Lied, 1775–1850." In *Women Making Music: The Western Art Tradition, 1150–1950*, edited by Jane Bowers and Judith Tick, 224–48. Urbana: University of Illinois Press, 1987.

Cowgill, Rachel E. "Savage, Jane." In *Grove Music Online*. Oxford University Press, 2001. https://doi.org/10.1093/gmo/9781561592630.article.24646.

Craw, Howard Allen, Matjaž Barbo, Barbara Garvey Jackson, and Bonnie Shaljean. "Dussek Family." In *Grove Music Online*. Oxford University Press, 2001. https://doi.org/10.1093/gmo/9781561592630.article.44229.

Cusick, Suzanne. *Francesca Caccini at the Medici Court: Music and the Circulation of Power*. Chicago: University of Chicago Press, 2009.

Edwards, J. Michele. "Bauer, Marion Eugénie." In *Grove Music Online*. Oxford University Press, 2001. https://doi.org/10.1093/gmo/9781561592630.article.02353.

Ernst, Pauer. *A Dictionary of Pianists and Composers for the Pianoforte*. London: Novello, 1896.

Fick, Kimary. "Feeling the Feminine, Forming the Masculine: Amateur Musicians and the Flute Sonatas of Anna Bon di Venezia (1738–?)." *Women and Music: A Journal of Gender and Culture* 24 (2020): 130–53.

Fitzlyon, April. *Maria Malibran: Diva of the Romantic Age*. London: Souvenir, 1987.

Forbes, Elizabeth. "Colbran, Isabella [Isabel]." In *Grove Music Online*. Oxford University Press, 2001. https://doi.org/10.1093/gmo/9781561592630.article.06067.

———. "Malibran [née García], Maria(-Felicia)." In *Grove Music Online*. Oxford University Press, 2009. https://doi.org/10.1093/gmo/9781561592630.article.17547.

Forkert, Annika. "Luise Adolpha Le Beau." MUGI. Musikvermittlung und Genderforschung: Lexikon und multimediale Präsentationen. Translated by Nancy Schuman. Hochschule für Musik und Theater Hamburg, 2018. https://mugi.hfmt-hamburg.de/receive/mugi_person_00000477.

Friedland, Bea. *Louise Farrenc, 1804–1875: Composer, Performer, Scholar*. Ann Arbor, MI: UMI Research Press, 1980.

Geliot, Christine. "Biography of Mel Bonis, 1858–1937." Mel Bonis Composer. Mel Bonis Association, 2020. https://www.mel-bonis.com/FR/Biographie/.

Godt, Irving. *Marianna Martines: A Woman Composer in the Vienna of Mozart and Haydn*. Edited with contributions by John A. Rice. Rochester, NY: University of Rochester Press, 2010.

Green, Jeffrey. *Samuel Coleridge-Taylor, a Musical Life*. New York: Routledge, 2011.

Grove Music Online. "Browne [Hughes], Harriet." Oxford University Press, 2004. https://doi.org/10.1093/gmo/9781561592630.article.54009.

Haefner, Jaymee. *One Stone to the Building: Henriette Renié's Life Through Her Works for Harp*. Bloomington, IN: AuthorHouse, 2017.

Hales, Douglas. *A Southern Family in White & Black: The Cuneys of Texas*. College Station: Texas A&M University Press, 2002.

Hettrick, Jane Schatkin. "Bon [Boni], Anna." In *Grove Music Online*. Oxford University Press, 2001. https://doi.org/10.1093/gmo/9781561592630.article.47932.

Hoffmann, Freia. "Blahetka, (Anne Marie) Leopoldine." In *Grove Music Online*. Oxford University Press, 2001. https://doi.org/10.1093/gmo/9781561592630.article.48542.

Joncus, Berta, and Vanessa Rogers. "'United voices formed the very perfection of harmony': Music and the Invention of Harriett Abrams (c. 1758–1821)." In *Celebrity: The Idiom of a Modern Era*, edited by Bärbel Czennia, 67–106. New York: AMS Press, 2013.

Jones, Charles K. *Francis Johnson (1792–1844): Chronicle of a Black Musician in Early Nineteenth-Century Philadelphia*. Bethlehem, PA: Lehigh University Press, 2006.

Kein, Sybil, ed. *Creole: The History and Legacy of Louisiana's Free People of Color*. Baton Rouge: Louisiana State University Press, 2000.

Kidd, Ronald R. "Schröter Family." In *Grove Music Online*. Oxford University Press, 2001. https://doi.org/10.1093/gmo/9781561592630.article.43982.

Kijas, Anna E. *The Life and Music of Teresa Carreño (1853–1917): A Guide to Research*. Middleton, WI: Music Library Association and A-R Editions, 2019.

Kimberling, Clark. "Henry Hart and His Family Orchestra." Henry Hart Project, 2010. https://faculty.evansville.edu/ck6/bstud/Supplement1.html.

King, Reyahn, Sukhdev Sandhu, James Walvin, and Jane Girdham. *Ignatius Sancho: An African Man of Letters*. London: National Portrait Gallery Publications, 1997.

Krebs, Harald, and Sharon Krebs. *Josephine Lang: Her Life and Songs*. Oxford: Oxford University Press, 2007.

LaMay, Thomasin. "Composing from the Throat: Madalena Casulana's *Primo libro de madrigali*, 1568." In *Musical Voices of Early Modern Women: Many-Headed Melodies*, edited by Thomasin LaMay, 365–98. Burlington, VT: Ashgate, 2005.

Largey, Michael D. *Vodou Nation: Haitian Art Music and Cultural Nationalism*. Chicago: University of Chicago Press, 2006.

Leandro de Souza, Vitor. "Maestro Anacleto de Medeiros: Cultura Negra, fronteiras e negociações." *Revista Mundo Livre* 3, no. 2 (2017): 80–92.

Letzter, Jacqueline, and Robert Adelson. *Women Writing Opera: Creativity and Controversy in the Age of the French Revolution*. Berkeley: University of California Press, 2001.

Liliuokalani, Queen of Hawaii. *Hawaii's Story by Hawaii's Queen*. Boston: Lothrop, Lee, and Shepard, 1898.

Magaldi, Cristina. "Gonzaga, (Francisca Edwiges Neves) Chiquinha." In *Grove Music Online*. Oxford University Press, 2001. https://doi.org/10.1093/gmo/9781561592630.article.45492.

Magner, Candace A. "Barbara Strozzi: My Life in 1600s Venice." Barbara Strozzi: La Virtuosissima Cantatrice, 2022. https://barbarastrozzi.com/a-brief-history/.

Maitland, J. A. Fuller, and Andrew Lamb. "Oury [née de Belleville], Anna Caroline." In *Grove Music Online*. Oxford University Press, 2001. https://doi.org/10.1093/gmo/9781561592630.article.20602.

McKee, Sally. *The Exile's Song: Edmond Dédé and the Unfinished Revolutions of the Atlantic World*. New Haven, CT: Yale University Press, 2017.

Meling, Lise Karin. "Maria Hester Park and Her Subscribers." In *Music by Subscription: Composers and Their Networks in the British Music-Publishing Trade, 1676–1820*, edited by Simon D. I. Fleming and Martin Perkins, 57–72. New York: Routledge, 2022.

Montesquiou, Odette de. *The Legend of Henriette Renié*. Edited by Jaymee Haefner. Translated by Robert Kilpatrick. Bloomington, IN: AuthorHouse, 2008.

Neuls-Bates, Carol. *Women in Music: An Anthology of Source Readings from the Middle Ages to the Present*. Revised edition. Boston: Northeastern University Press, 1996.

Olson, Judith E. "Le Beau, Luise Adolpha." In *Grove Music Online*. Oxford University Press, 2005. https://doi.org/10.1093/gmo/9781561592630.article.2019862.

Orledge, Robert. "Tailleferre, Germaine." In *Grove Music Online*. Oxford University Press, 2001. https://doi.org/10.1093/gmo/9781561592630.article.27390.

Pita, Laura. "Carreño, (María) Teresa." In *Grove Music Online*. Oxford University Press, 2015. https://doi.org/10.1093/gmo/9781561592630.article.A2282327.

Potter, Caroline. "Boulanger, (Juliette) Nadia." In *Grove Music Online*. Oxford University Press, 2002. https://doi.org/10.1093/gmo/9781561592630.article.03705.

Porter, Cecelia Hopkins. *Five Lives in Music: Women Performers, Composers, and Impresarios from the Baroque to the Present*. Urbana: University of Illinois Press, 2012.

Quetin, Laurine. "Hortense." In *Grove Music Online*. Oxford University Press, 2001. https://doi.org/10.1093/gmo/9781561592630.article.13380.

Reich, Nancy B. *Clara Schumann: The Artist and the Woman.* Revised edition. Ithaca, NY: Cornell University Press, 2001.

———. Introduction to *Songs* by Louise Reichardt, vii–xix. New York: Da Capo Press, 1981.

Rosand, Ellen, and Beth L. Glixon. "Strozzi, Barbara." In *Grove Music Online.* Oxford University Press, 2002. https://doi.org/10.1093/gmo/9781561592630.article.26987.

Rose, Maria. "Hélène de Montgeroult and the Art of Singing Well on the Piano." *Women and Music: A Journal of Gender and Culture* 5 (2001): 99–124.

Rushton, Julian, Julie Anne Sadie, Robert Adelson, and Jacqueline Letzter. "Candeille, (Amélie) [Emilie] Julie." In *Grove Music Online.* Oxford University Press, 2014. https://doi.org/10.1093/gmo/9781561592630.article.04725.

Ryder, Georgia A. "Harlem Renaissance Ideals in the Music of Robert Nathaniel Dett." In *Black Music in the Harlem Renaissance*, edited by Samuel A. Floyd Jr., 55–70. Westport, CT: Greenwood, 1990.

Sadie, Julie Anne. "Ménétou, Françoise-Charlotte de Senneterre, Mlle de." In *Grove Music Online.* Oxford University Press, 2004. https://doi.org/10.1093/gmo/9781561592630.article.54054.

———. "Pinel, Julie." In *Grove Music Online.* Oxford University Press, 2001. https://doi.org/10.1093/gmo/9781561592630.article.2021283.

Sadownik, Stephanie. "The *Lieder* of Emilie Mayer (1812–1883)." DMA diss., Arizona State University, 2020.

Shewbert, Sarah Grace. "Marion Bauer's 'Completely Musical Life' (1882–1955): An American Composer's Essential Creative Works and Contributions to Twentieth-Century Music." PhD diss., University of Washington, 2014.

Snyder, Jean E. *Harry T. Burleigh: From the Spiritual to the Harlem Renaissance.* Urbana: University of Illinois Press, 2016.

Southern, Eileen. "Davis, Gussie Lord." In *Grove Music Online.* Oxford University Press, 2013. https://doi.org/10.1093/gmo/9781561592630.article.A2234921.

Sweet, Nanora. "Hemans [née Browne], Felicia Dorothea (1793–1835), poet." In *Oxford Dictionary of National Biography.* Oxford University Press, 2004. https://doi.org/10.1093/ref:odnb/12888.

Todd, R. Larry. *Fanny Hensel: The Other Mendelssohn.* New York: Oxford University Press, 2010.

Tsou, Judy. "Bonis, Mélanie (Hélène)." In *Grove Music Online.* Oxford University Press, 2012. https://doi.org/10.1093/gmo/9781561592630.article.45497.

Tsou, Judy, and William Cheng. "Puget, Loïsa." In *Grove Music Online.* Oxford University Press, 2012. https://doi.org/10.1093/gmo/9781561592630.article.22525.

Vega, Aurelio de la. "White Lafitte, José." In *Grove Music Online.* Oxford University Press, 2001. https://doi.org/10.1093/gmo/9781561592630.article.30221.

Walker-Hill, Helen, ed. *Black Women Composers: A Century of Piano Music (1893–1990).* Bryn Mawr, PA: Hildegard Publishing, 1992.

———. "Music by Black Women Composers at the American Research Center." *American Research Center Journal* 2 (1992): 23–52.

Webber, Rachel. Program Note to "Whilst shepherds watch'd their flocks by night," by Jane Savage. Oxford: Oxford University Press, 2020.

Wollenberg, Susan. "Barthélémon [married name Henslow], Cecilia Maria." In *Oxford Dictionary of National Biography.* Oxford University Press, 2006. https://doi.org/10.1093/ref:odnb/61854.

Wright, Josephine. "Violinist José White in Paris, 1855–1875." *Black Music Research Journal* 10, no. 2 (Autumn 1990): 213–32.

Yelloly, Margaret. "'The Ingenious Miss Turner': Elizabeth Turner (d. 1756), Singer, Harpsichordist and Composer." *Early Music* 33, no. 1 (2005): 65–79.

Index

Abrams, Harriett
  biography of, 313
  A Smile and a Tear, *91*
  The Three Sighs: Sorrow, Hope, & Bliss, *89*
Aldridge, Amanda Ira
  biography of, 313
  Carnival: Frolic, *62*
  Carnival: Pierrette, *33, 172*
  Three Pictures from Syria: The Desert Patrol, *128*

Barthélemon, Cecilia Maria
  biography of, 314
  Keyboard Sonata, Op. 3: Rondo alla hornpipe, *145*
Bauer, Marion
  biography of, 314
  Prelude No. 4, Op. 15, *44*
Beach, Amy
  biography of, 314
  Piano Concerto, Op. 45: Allegro moderato, *14–16*
Beauharnais, Hortense de
  L'attente, *21*
  L'aveu, *108*
  biography of, 315
  Le bon chevalier, *116*
  Je l'ai reçu, *13*
  Les jeunes rêves d'amour, *110*
  Lay de l'exil, *118*
  M'entends-tu, *134–35*
  Ne m'oubliez pas!, *96*
  L'orage, *14*
  Plus n'aimerai, *120*
  Le prisonnier, *58*
  La sentinelle, *126*

Blahetka, Leopoldine
  biography of, 315
  Erinnerungen an Holland, Op. 33, *201*
Bologne, Joseph
  biography of, 315
  Sonata No. 1, Op. 1a: Allegro, *118*
  Sonata No. 2: Aria con variatione, *59*
  Sonata No. 3: [Allegro], *59*
  String Quartet No. 1, Op. 1: Allegro assai, *119*
  String Quartet No. 1, Op. 1: Rondeau, *210*
  String Quartet No. 2, Op. 1: Rondeau, *127*
  String Quartet No. 4, Op. 1: Allegro moderato, *30–31, 105, 141*
  String Quartet No. 4, Op. 1: Rondeau, *251–53*
  Symphony No. 1, Op. 11: Allegro, *73–74*
  Symphony No. 1, Op. 11: Allegro assai, *128*
  Symphony No. 1, Op. 11: Andante, *207–8*
Bon, Anna
  biography of, 316
  Sonata No. 2, Op. 1: Allegro, *31–32*
  Sonata No. 2, Op. 1: Largo, *66, 199*
  Sonata No. 4, Op. 1: Allegro moderato, *195–96*
  Sonata No. 5, Op. 1: Allegro, *193*
  Sonata No. 6, Op. 1: Adagio, *196*
  Sonata No. 6, Op. 1: Allegro, *198*

Bonis, Mélanie
  biography of, 316
  Carillon mystique, Op. 31, *75*
  Cinq pièces pour piano: Gai printemps, *60*
  Viennoise, Op. 8, *188, 207*
Boulanger, Nadia
  biography of, 316
  Three Pieces for Cello and Piano: No. 3, *42–43*
Browne, Harriet
  Ave Sanctissima, *102*
  biography of, 317
  The Lyre of the Sea Cave, *170*
Burleigh, Harry Thacker
  biography of, 317
  Sometimes I feel like a Motherless Child, *22*

Caccini, Francesca
  biography of, 317
  Chi é costei, *81*
Candeille, Julie
  biography of, 318
  Romance de Catherine, *132*
  Sonata No. 1, Op. 1: Allegro, *235–43*
Carreño, Teresa
  biography of, 318
  Deux élégies, Op. 17: Plainte!, *160*
  Deux élégies, Op. 18: Partie!, *13, 47–48, 106*
  Deux esquisses italiennes, Op. 33: Venise, *163–64*
  Le ruisseau, Op. 29, *172*
  Six morceaux de salon, Op. 26: Un bal en rêve, *34–35, 140, 185*
  String Quartet in B Minor: Andante, *304–11*
  Trois morceaux de salon, Op. 25: Le Printemps, *94*
  Trois morceaux de salon, Op. 28: Un rêve en mer, *42*
Casulana, Maddalena
  biography of, 318
  Cinta di fior un giorno, *35*

Chaminade, Cécile
  Air italien, Op. 170, *20*
  Album des enfants, Op. 123: Gavotte, *209*
  Album des enfants, Op. 123: Intermezzo, *137*
  biography of, 319
Colbran, Isabella
  biography of, 319
  Ombre amene, amiche piante, *104*
  Più bella Aurora, *65, 183*
  So che un sogno è la speranza, *92, 115*
Coleridge-Taylor, Samuel
  African Dances, Op. 58: No. 1, *153–54*
  Ballade, Op. 4, *49–50, 155, 162–63*
  biography of, 319–20
  Fantasiestücke, Op. 5, *43–44*
  Four Characteristic Waltzes, Op. 22: Valse de la Reine, *23–24, 187*
  Three Humoresques, Op. 31: No. 1, *166*

Davis, Gussie
  biography of, 320
  Irene, Good Night, *151*
Dédé, Edmond
  biography of, 320
  Chicago, *154, 166*
  Françoise et Tortillard: Duo, *168–69*
  Méphisto masqué: Introduction, *209*
Dédé, Eugène
  biography of, 321
  Douleur et gaîté, *64*
  Miaou!! Miaou!!!, Op. 238, *214–15*
Dett, Robert Nathaniel
  biography of, 321
  In the Bottoms: Honey-Humoresque, *111*
  In the Bottoms: Prelude: Night, *34, 296–97*
  Listen to the Lambs, *152*
Dussek, Sophia
  biography of, 321

In April When Prim Roses, *69*
Sonata No. 3, Op. 2: Rondo,
    261–65
Sonata No. 3, Op. 3: Andantino,
    215–16
Spanish Boleros, *126*
Variations on "Beauty in Tears,"
    116
Variations on "In my cottage in a
    wood," *88*
Variations on "Lewie Gordon,"
    93
Ye Banks & Braes, *289–91*
Duval, Mademoiselle
    biography of, 322
    Les caractères de l'Amour: Act 1,
        Scene 1, Air Leandre, *82*
    Les caractères de l'Amour: Prologue,
        Air pour les genies, *21*, *198*

Elie, Justin
    biography of, 322
    Tropical Dance No. 2, *73*, *168*

Farrenc, Louise
    biography of, 322
    Étude No. 2, Op. 42, *16–17*
    Étude No. 4, Op. 42, *181*
    Étude No. 6, Op. 50, *150*
    Étude No. 12, Op. 41, *158–59*
    Sonata No. 2, Op. 39: Finale,
        272–85
    Trio, Op. 45: Allegro deciso, *164–65*, *178*, *202*
    Trio, Op. 45: Andante, *211*
    Trio, Op. 45: Finale, *184*
    Trio, Op. 45: Scherzo, *197*

Gonzaga, Chiquinha
    Ai que broma!, *167*
    Alerta!, *108*
    Bijou, *74*
    biography of, 323
    Carlos Gomes, *32*
    Carrapatoso, *142*
    Chi, *173*
    Dansa das fadas, *129–30*
    Fado das Tricanas de Coimbra, *68*
Goodwin, Anna Gardner
    biography of, 323
    Cuba Libre, *68*
    The Educational Congress March,
        106

Hare, Maud Cuney
    Aurore Pradère, *104–5*, *173*
    biography of, 323
    Quand mo-té jeune, *73*
Hart, Henry
    biography of, 324
    On the Beautiful Lake Erie, *209*
Hensel, Fanny Mendelssohn
    biography of, 324
    Vier Lieder für das Pianoforte, Op.
        2: No. 4, *174*

Jacquet de La Guerre, Élisabeth
    biography of, 324
    Violin Sonata No. 1: Aria, *80*
    Violin Sonata No. 1: Presto, *194–95*
    Violin Sonata No. 2: Presto, *52*
    Violin Sonata No. 5: Aria, *109–10*
    Violin Sonata No. 5: Courante,
        82–83
    Violin Sonata No. 5: Lent, *126*
    Violin Sonata No. 6: Adagio,
        193–94
    Violin Sonata No. 6: Aria, *119*
    Violin Sonata No. 6: Presto, *81*
Johnson, Francis
    biography of, 325
    A Collection of New Cotillions:
        Augustus, *117*
    A Collection of New Cotillions: Ford,
        58
    A Collection of New Cotillions:
        Francis, *97*, *98*

Lambert, Sydney
    biography of, 325
    Ninon, *176*
    Transports joyeux, Op. 16, *65*, *105*

Lang, Josephine
  Arie: All' mein Leben bist du, *33*, *116*
  biography of, 325
  Blick' nach oben, *48–49*
  Danse infernale, Op. 46, *119*
  Dort hoch auf jenem Berge, *80*
  Festmarsch, Op. 31, *129*
  Frühzeitiger Frühling, Op. 6, *24–25*, *146–47*
  Hochzeits-Marsch, Op. 42, *20*, *96–97*
  Nähe des Geliebten, Op. 5, *143–44*
  Wein' aus deine Freude, *159*
  Der Winter, Op. 15, *120*
Larkins, Ida M.
  biography of, 326
  Wild Flowers, *103–4*
Le Beau, Luise Adolpha
  biography of, 326
  Elegie, Op. 44, *120*
  Violin Sonata No. 1, Op. 10: Allegro con fuoco, *145*, *206–7*
Lebrun, Franziska
  biography of, 326
  Sonata No. 1, Op. 1: Allegro, *132*
  Sonata No. 3, Op. 1: Rondeau, *266–71*
  Sonata No. 4, Op. 2: Rondo allegro assai, *82*
  Sonata No. 5, Op. 1: Allegro, *115*
  Sonata No. 5, Op. 1: Rondeau, *93*, *153*
  Sonata No. 6, Op. 1: Rondeau, *254–60*
Leonarda, Isabella
  biography of, 327
  Non scintilate frigide, Op. 11, *199*
  O sylvæ, ò montes, ò garruli fontes, Op. 11, *53*
  Sonata No. 3, Op. 16: Adagio-Presto, *83–84*
  Sonata No. 3, Op. 16: Largo, *121*
  Sonata No. 4, Op. 16: Prestissimo, *109*
  Sonata No. 5, Op. 16: Adagio, *98*
  Sonata No. 6, Op. 16, *62–63*
  Sonata No. 7, Op. 16: Largo, *121–22*
  Sonata No. 9, Op. 16: Presto, *200–201*
  Sonata No. 11, Op. 16: Allegro, *134*
  Ubi es ò Domine, Op. 11, *69*
Liliuokalani
  Aloha Oe, *123*
  biography of, 327

Malibrán, María
  Le batelier, *64*
  biography of, 327
  En soupirant, *102–3*
  L'indifférence, *182–83*
  Nuova tarantella, *128*
Martines, Marianna
  biography of, 328
  Sonata in A Major: Rondo, *208*
  Sonata in A Major: Tempo di minuetto, *88–89*
  Sonata in E Major: Allegro, *89*
  Sonata in G Major: Allegro assai, *90*
Mayer, Emilie
  biography of, 328
  Humoreske No. 3, Op. 41, *84*
  Der Neugierige, Op. 10, *186*
  Das Schlüsselloch im Herzen, *146*
  Valse, Op. 32, *184–85*
  Violin Sonata, Op. 17: Adagio non troppo, *79*
Medeiros, Anacleto de
  biography of, 328
  Terna saudade, *133*
Ménétou, Françoise-Charlotte de Senneterre
  Ah! Si vous sçaviez mes compagnes, *79*
  biography of, 329
Montgeroult, Hélène de
  biography of, 329

Sonata No. 1, Op. 1: Prestissimo, *221–28*

Oury, Anna Caroline
  biography of, 329
  Valse brillante, *176–77*

Paradis, Maria Theresia von
  biography of, 330
  Da eben seinem Lauf vollbracht, *127, 206*
  Erinnerung ans Schicksal, *51–52*
  Das Gärtnerliedchen aus dem Siegwart, *150–51*
  Wohl und immer wohl dem Mann, *133*

Park, Maria Hester
  biography of, 330
  Sonata, Op. 7: Allegro spirito, *229–34*

Parke, Maria Frances
  biography of, 330
  Sonata No. 3, Op. 1: Allegro, *212*

Pinel, Julie
  biography of, 331
  Buvons Lucas, *98*
  Que Tircis est charmant, *182*
  Ruisseaux suspendez vôtre cours, *90–91*

Puget, Loïsa
  biography of, 331
  Le bon curé patience, *135–36*
  La chanson du charbonnier, *130*

Reichardt, Louise
  biography of, 331
  Erinnrung am Bach, *111*
  Giusto Amor, *79, 158*
  Heymdal, *122*
  Hier liegt ein Spielmann begraben, *72*
  Ich wollt' ein Sträuslein binden, *60*
  Der Mond, *103*
  Nach Sevilla, *140–41*
  Schifferlied, *88*
  Unruhiger Schlaf, *22–23*
  Vaters Klage, *38–39*

Renié, Henriette
  biography of, 332
  Danse des lutins, *29*
  Trio for Harp, Violin, and Cello: Andante, *41*

Rogers, Clara Kathleen
  biography of, 332
  The Clover Blossoms, Op. 10, *47, 143*
  Scherzo, Op. 15, *142*
  Spring, Op. 20, *189*
  Violin Sonata, Op. 25: Allegro, *74–75, 136–37, 208*
  Violin Sonata, Op. 25: Più lento molto sostenuto, *39–40*

Sancho, Ignatius
  biography of, 332–33
  Dutchess of Devonshires Reel, *181*
  Lord Dalkeiths Reel, *118*
  Minuet No. 5, *216–17*
  Trip to Dilington, *97*

Savage, Jane
  biography of, 333
  Sonata No. 5, Op. 2: Minuet, *214*

Schröter, Corona
  biography of, 333
  Der Brautschmuck, *90*

Schumann, Clara
  biography of, 333
  Fuga No. 1, Op. 16, *300–302*
  Piano Trio, Op. 17: Scherzo, *25*

Sirmen, Maddalena Laura
  biography of, 334
  Sonata No. 2, Op. 1: Menuetto smorfioso and Trio, *246–48*

Strozzi, Barbara
  biography of, 334
  Che si può fare, Op. 8, *40, 292–95*

Tailleferre, Germaine
  biography of, 334
  String Quartet: Final, *38*

Turner, Elizabeth
 biography of, 335
 Lesson No. 1: Allegro, *196–97*
 Lesson No. 1: Minuetto, *13–14*, *218*
 Lesson No. 1: Tambourine, *117*
 Lesson No. 3: Minuetto affetuoso, *110*

Verger, Virginie Morel-du
 biography of, 335
 La disperata, *99*, *159*

White, José
 biography of, 335
 Etude No. 1, Op. 33, *29–30*
 Zamacueca, Op. 30, *177*